SHAW ISLAND LIBRARY

Do-Ho Suh

Lisa G. Corrin and Miwon Kwon

Serpentine Gallery, London
23 April – 26 May 2002

Seattle Art Museum/Seattle Asian Art Museum
10 August – 1 December 2002

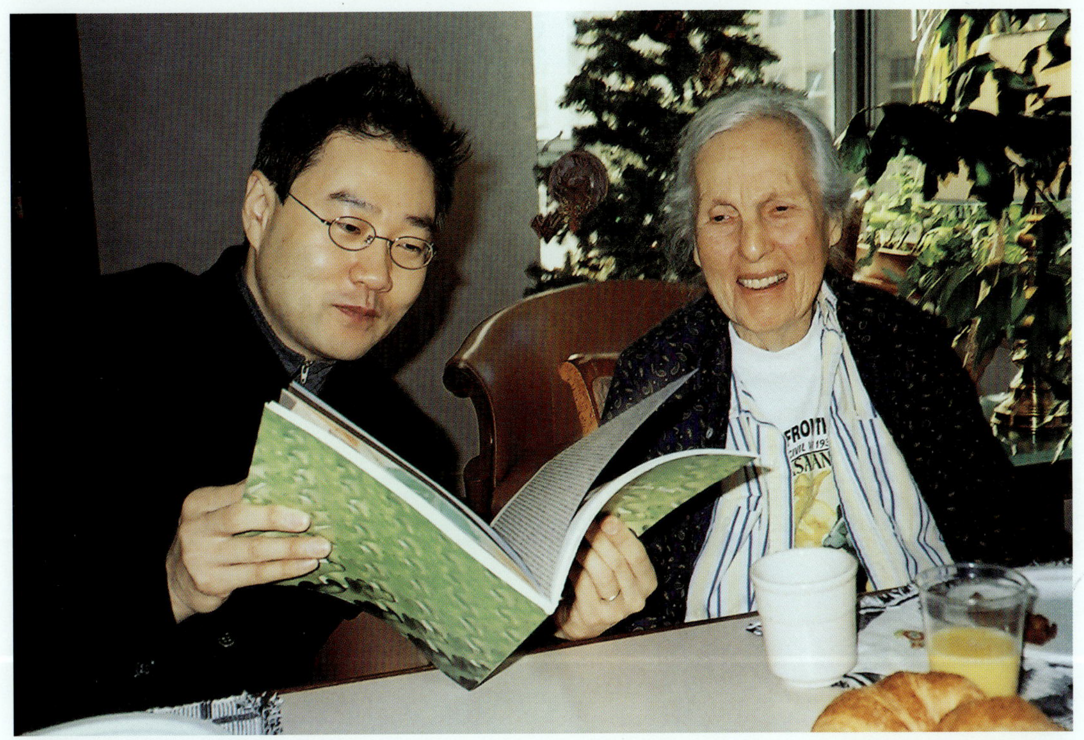

Do-Ho Suh with Anne Gerber

Photo: Michael McCafferty, 2001

The Anne Gerber Fund was initiated by friends of Anne Gerber, Seattle collector, philanthropist and arts community leader, in recognition of her support for contemporary art in the Northwest region. The Fund supports the Anne Gerber Biennial, a series enabling the Seattle Art Museum to present international art of our time to a broad public, such as this exhibition of the works of Do-Ho Suh.

Who Am We? (Multi) 2000
Courtesy of the artist and Lehmann Maupin Gallery, New York

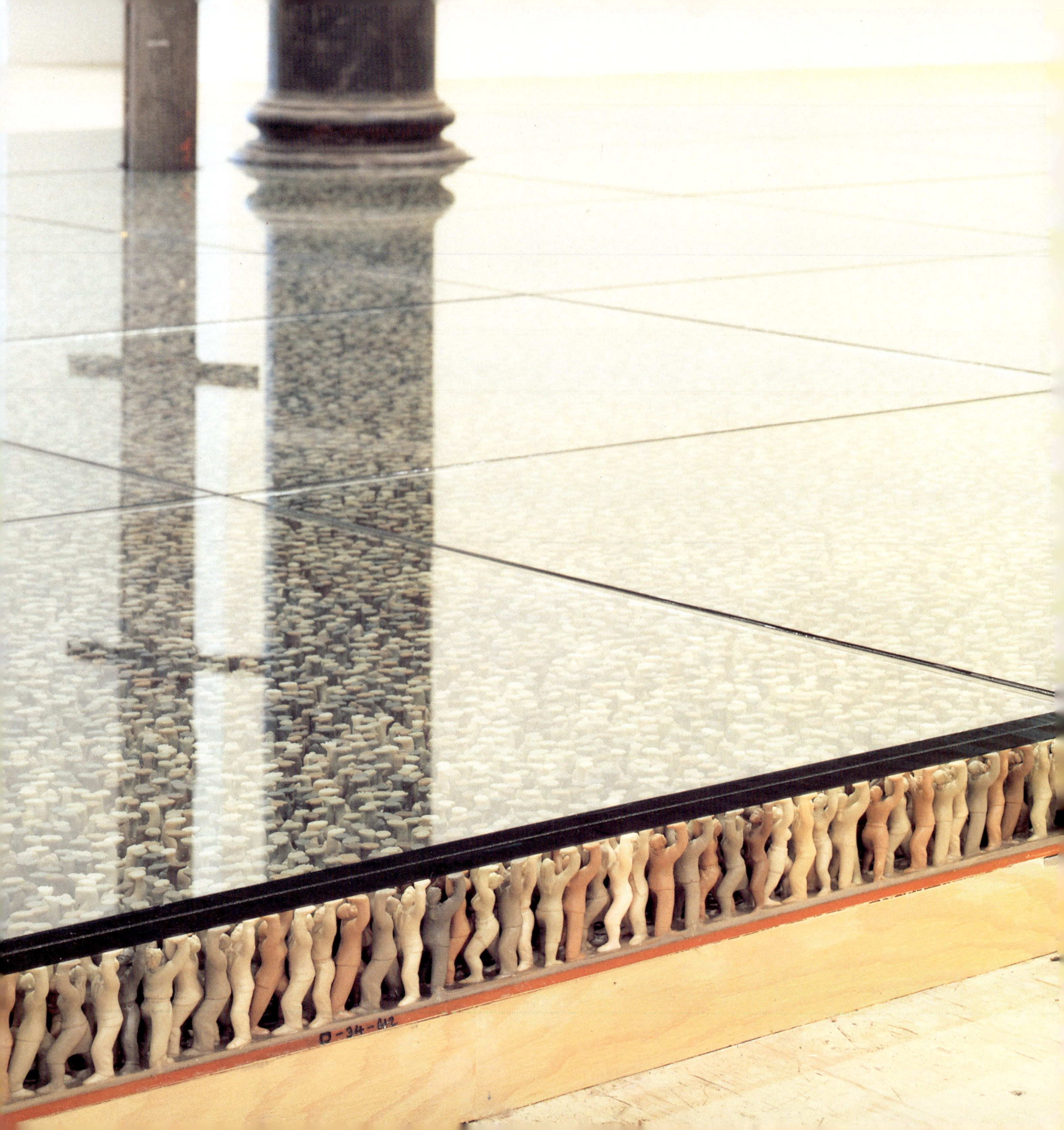

Directors' Foreword

The Serpentine Gallery and the Seattle Art Museum are pleased to collaborate to present the first survey exhibition in Europe and the United States of the work of Korean-born artist Do-Ho Suh. His well known installation *Seoul Home/L.A. Home/New York Home/Baltimore Home/London Home/Seattle Home*, a spectacular celadon-green fabric sculpture modelled on his childhood home, has, since its completion in 1999, travelled to Los Angeles, Baltimore, New York, and now London and Seattle. Its migration between continents is charted through its constantly evolving title that now includes each of these cities and will continue to be augmented with future sitings. *Some/One*, fabricated entirely of shiny army-style dog tags and installed at the Whitney Museum of American Art at Philip Morris in New York in 2001, brought the artist significant acclaim. It appeared in a second version as part of a presentation of Suh's work, together with that of Michael Joo, in the Korean Pavilion at the 49th Venice Biennale in 2001.

Born in Korea in 1962, Suh currently lives and works in New York City. In his late twenties, he moved to the United States to continue his training as an artist, earning a Bachelor's degree in painting from the Rhode Island School of Design in 1994 and a Master's degree in sculpture from Yale University in 1997. Suh is perhaps best known for his sculptures that comprise numerous identical objects including a 'camouflage' floor supported by thousands of miniature plastic figures, and wallpaper representing some 37,000 tiny portraits from his high school yearbooks. Through this repetition of forms, the artist refers to the complex relationship between the individual and the collective, a theme that is informed by his particular cultural context.

Equally important is Suh's group of diaphanous silk and nylon architectural installations based upon full-scale sections of the interiors of the homes in which he has lived, both in Korea and the United States. These works function as transitional objects enabling Suh to negotiate what he refers to as his 'transcultural displacement', as he migrates between his country of origin and his 'foreign' home in the U.S. Suh invites viewers to step into and move through the individual 'rooms' and 'corridors' to experience these dislocated personal spaces first-hand.

The Serpentine Gallery and the Seattle Art Museum would like to thank Do-Ho Suh for the time and consideration he has given to this exhibition and for recreating and adapting a number of works for each venue. We are also grateful to the artist's assistants in Korea, Jin-O Kwon and Sung-Ha Hwang, who assisted with the installation of the exhibition. The artist's parents Min-Za Chung and

Floor 1997–2000
Courtesy of the artist and Lehmann Maupin Gallery, New York

Se-Ok Suh, along with Yeon-Hui Liu, Young-Ki Sul, Sa Li Za, Dr Young-Sook Han, Miwon Kwon, Sowon Kwon, Tia Shin and Kaori Enjoji, have provided invaluable support to the artist and have played crucial roles in realizing this exhibition.

As ever, we are particularly grateful to the museums and private collectors who have generously lent works to the exhibition, including The Museum of Contemporary Art, Los Angeles; the Samsung Museum of Modern Art, Seoul; Estēe Lauder Companies; Barbara Goldfarb; Ninah and Michael Lynne; and David Teiger. We also would like to thank Rachel Lehmann and David Maupin of Lehmann Maupin Gallery, New York, and their gallery staff, especially Juliet Gray, Vera Brunner-Sung and Ingrid Lee, whose assistance has been invaluable.

The exhibition was selected by Lisa G. Corrin, Deputy Director of Art/Jon and Mary Shirley Curator of Modern and Contemporary Art at the Seattle Art Museum, and former Chief Curator at the Serpentine Gallery, in close consultation with the artist. In Seattle, her successful partnership with Jay Xu, Foster Foundation Curator of Chinese Art, in particular, has enhanced public appreciation of the cultural context of Suh's work by presenting the fabric installations at the Seattle Asian Art Museum in Volunteer Park.

Lisa G. Corrin and Miwon Kwon have contributed insightful texts to this catalogue, and we are extremely grateful to them as well as to Leigh Markopolous, Assistant Director at the CCAC Wattis Institute for Contemporary Arts, San Francisco and former Exhibition Organizer at the Serpentine Gallery, and Helen Wire for their editorial contributions. Herman Lelie has designed this handsome catalogue on the occasion of the exhibition.

The Serpentine is delighted to collaborate once again with Bloomberg, especially Lex Fenwick and Patti Harris, who are the sponsors of the exhibition in London, and whose generosity has been crucial in bringing these works to the Gallery. Jemma Read at Bloomberg and Rebecca King Lassman of Act IV have supported the Serpentine's wish to present the exhibition in London to the highest standard and we are enormously appreciative of their continuing dedication to the Gallery. We also gratefully acknowledge the valuable support this exhibition has received from David and Danielle Ganek.

At the Seattle Art Museum, Do-Ho Suh's exhibition is presented as part of the Anne Gerber Biennial series, a programme that underscores the Museum's ongoing commitment to the art of our time internationally. It is especially appropriate that this project is being presented as one exhibition in the Museum's two sites – downtown and at the Seattle Asian Art Museum where it will be experienced along with Grandfather's House, a recreation of traditional Korean domestic architecture of the type that has had such a profound influence on the work of Do-Ho Suh. One of the Seattle Art Museum's greatest strengths is its wide-ranging collection of Asian art. This exhibition encourages visitors to the Museum to connect contemporary art to the art of the past and to acknowledge Suh's contribution to a continuum of living cultural traditions. The exhibition is supported in Seattle by the Anne Gerber Exhibition Fund. Generous support was also contributed by Maryann and Henry James. Additional funding has been provided by the Wallace-Reader's Digest Funds, strengthening the Museum's programming and community partnerships. The Seattle Art Museum also wishes to thank the Consul General of the Republic of Korea Moon Byng-rok, Consul Shin Yong-gi and the Consulate General of the Republic of Korea in Seattle for their enthusiastic support of the project.

Finally, we would like to thank all of our colleagues in both institutions for their commitment to this exhibition. At the Serpentine Gallery, many people have contributed to the success of Do-Ho Suh's exhibition: Rochelle Steiner, Chief Curator; Claire Fitzsimmons, Exhibition Organiser; Leigh Markopolous, former Exhibition Organiser; Mike Gaughan, Gallery Manager, and the installation team; Sally Tallant, Head of Education Programming; Rose Dempsey, Press Officer; Louise McKinney and Natasha Roach, Development Managers.

At the Seattle Art Museum, additional thanks are due to the following individuals. Curatorial Division: Chiyo Ishikawa, Chief Curator of Collections/Curator of European Painting and Sculpture; Zora Hutlova Foy, Manager of Exhibitions and Curatorial Publications; Tara Young, Assistant Curator of Modern and Contemporary Art; Susan Bartlett, Exhibitions and Collections Coordinator; and Liz Andres, Curatorial Coordinator. Director's Office: Victoria Moreland, Director of Community Affairs. Education: Sarah Loudon, Senior Museum Educator, Asian Art Programs. Museum Services: Michael McCafferty, Exhibition Designer; Chris Manojlovic, Associate Exhibition Designer; and Lauren Tucker, Associate Registrar. External Affairs: Maryann Jordan, Deputy Director for Strategic Planning and External Affairs, and her entire staff including John Ferguson, Facilities Marketing Manager.

Julia Peyton-Jones
Director, Serpentine Gallery

Mimi Gardner Gates
The Illsley Ball Nordstrom Director, Seattle Art Museum

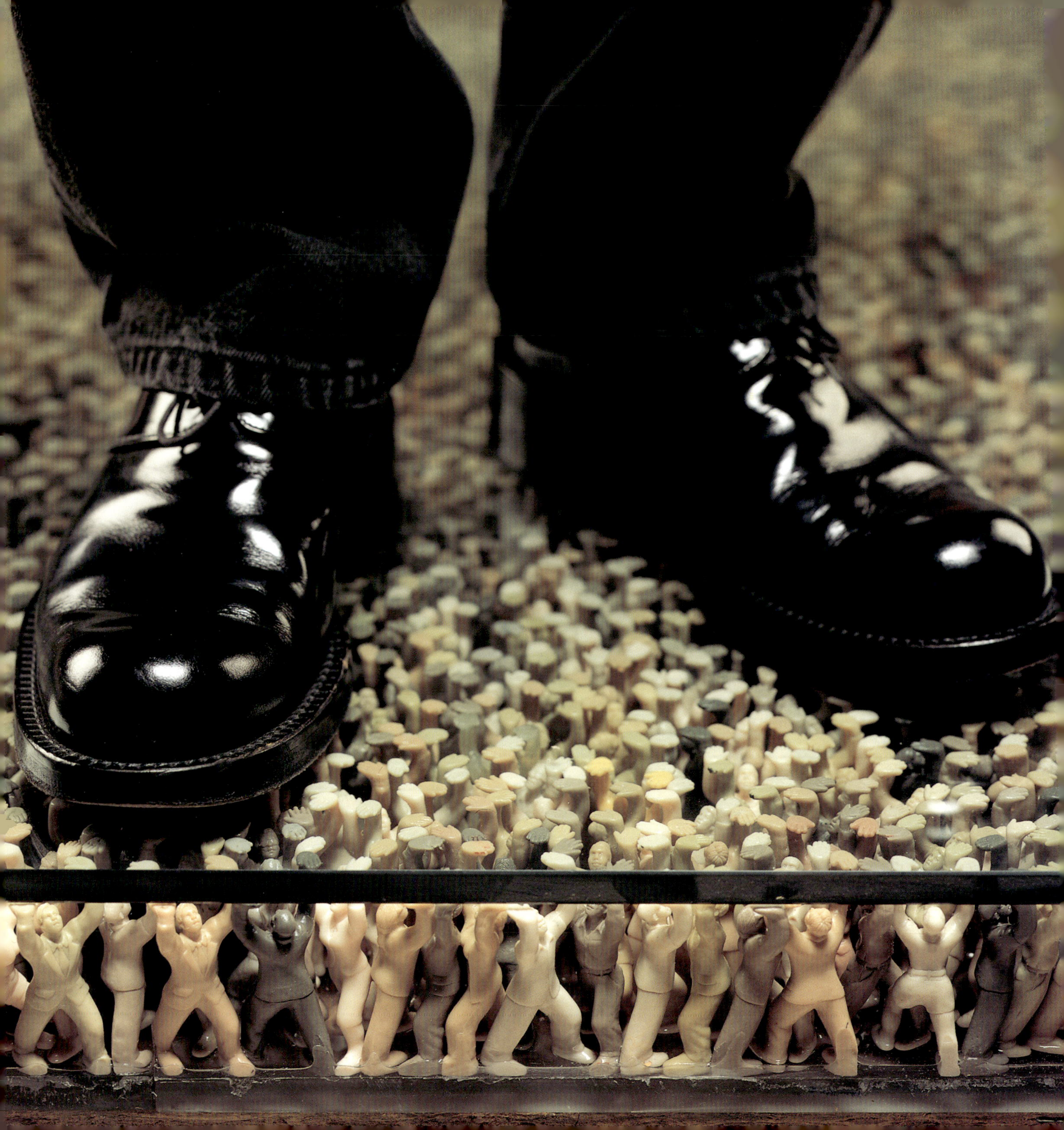

The Other Otherness: The Art of Do-Ho Suh

Miwon Kwon

Take One: Detailing Minimalism

Sculptures to walk on, to inhabit, and possibly to wear, Do-Ho Suh's projects of the past several years seem to implicate the body of the viewer in various ways. *Floor* (1997–2000) is an expansive platform covered with thick glass plates. Visitors find themselves stepping on it before they realize that they are treading on an artwork. Two works with cumbersome location titles – *Seoul Home/ L.A. Home/New York Home/Baltimore Home/London Home/Seattle Home* (1999) and *348 West 22nd St., Apt. A, New York, NY 10011 at Rodin Gallery, Seoul/Tokyo Opera City Art Gallery/ Serpentine Gallery, London/Biennale of Sydney/Seattle Art Museum* (2000) – are custom-fitted, tent-like casings of the artist's own domestic spaces. The former is of his childhood home in Korea, the latter is of his apartment in the United States. *Who Am We?* (2000), an installation of artist-designed wallpaper, transforms existing walls or rooms into a field of barely discernible faces – 37,000 of them collected from the artist's high school yearbooks – in a seemingly endless repetition. The installation complicates the stability of the room/gallery in a different way by enlivening it with the unsettling and uncanny presence of strangers. Finally, *High School Uni-Form* (1996) consists of 60, or in larger versions 300, Korean schoolboy's jackets sewn together as one, and *Some/One* (2001) is a majestic metal robe composed of thousands of stainless steel army-style 'dog tags'. Both are hollow shells of highly formal attire referencing a military body.

In part because of the formal reduction and visual simplicity of these works, but more in response to their engagement of the viewer's body, many critics have drawn connections between Suh's practice and Minimalism. Among the most thoughtful is Janet Kraynak, who has written:

> Collectively, Suh's artworks perform an extraordinary elaboration upon the spatial expansion of the sculptural object initiated in postwar art by Minimalism. Conceived as a field rather than a discrete thing, sculpture in Minimalism became experiential, temporal and interactive, directly addressing the perceptual conditions of the beholder. Minimalism's transformation of the terms of viewing is both recognized and dramatized in Suh's art in its continual tweaking of the conditions of beholding.[1]

Expanding the parameters of aesthetic experience to include the relational dynamic between space, body and object, and provoking the consciousness of the viewer to take in the entirety of the exhibition condition, are indeed consistent with attributes of Minimalism's challenge to the idealist formalism of

Floor (detail) 1997–2000
Courtesy of the artist and Lehmann Maupin Gallery, New York

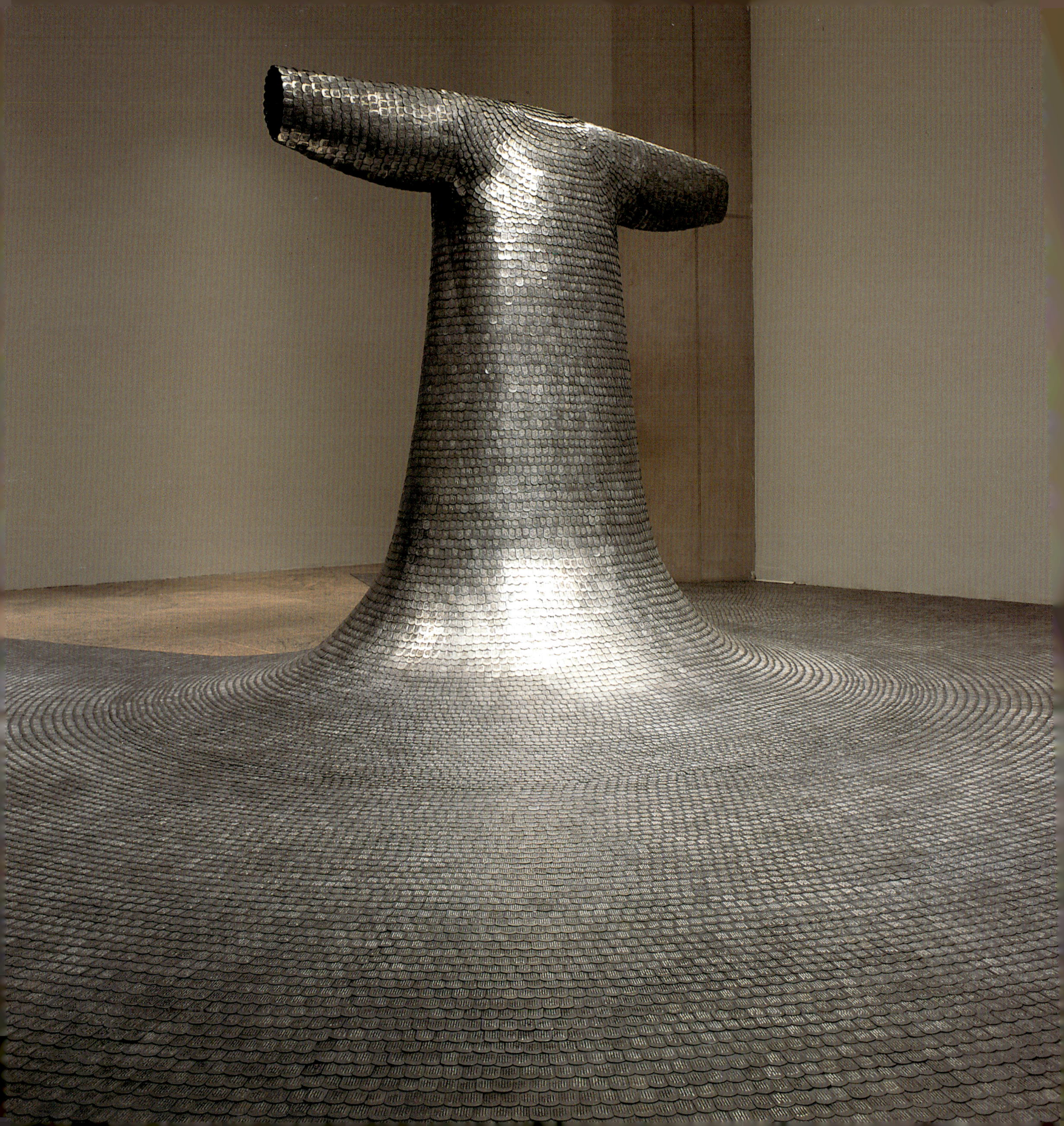

Greenbergian modernism.[2] And these concerns have defined the framework within which Suh has pursued his thematic interest in the binding of individuality and collectivity, identity and anonymity, memory and space, mobility and home, and the transportability of site-specific art.

Less recognized, however, is how Suh's work simultaneously develops an antithetical aspect to Minimalism. The seductive details of his installations captivate and capture the viewer in a way that deflects his/her attention *away* from the broader conditions of the presentation site. In *Floor*, for example, the viewer realizes at some point that underneath the glass surface upon which s/he is walking are countless tiny plastic figures apparently holding up the weight of the floor and those standing on it. (Bending over the edge of the floor yields a sectional view of the work.) Similarly, when the viewer moves extremely close to the wall in *Who Am We?*, s/he notices that the subtly textured pattern on it is comprised of thousands of miniscule portraits. In both instances, what starts as a spatial, public experience, in which you track yourself moving through the given space, noticing certain architectural incidents – like the floor or the wall – and watching others in relation to yourself, becomes an amusing moment of private discovery. Such revelations alter the experience of these works irreversibly. Once the details are perceived, they cannot be unknown; they trump the phenomenological aspects of the installations. Thus, what you initially see is *not* what you get in much of Suh's work.[3] On close inspection there is always an arresting find.

The use of the words public and private to characterize the divergent ways in which Suh's work activates the viewer's experience is not accidental. These terms were put into play precisely by Minimalist discourse, most explicitly by American artist Robert Morris in relation to the role of size and scale of 'useless three-dimensional things'. In 'Notes on Sculpture, Part II' (1966), he theorized that the human body functions as a constant through and against which the world of objects, from the ornament to the monument, finds meaning. An object's size as it diminishes in relation to the body renders the encounter between the two an intimate private experience; conversely, an increase in the object's size in relation to the body renders the experience public. This range of experience from intimate to public is a function of a spatial negotiation. For Morris, objects that require close inspection squeeze out space: a small object is 'essentially closed, spaceless, compressed, and exclusive' because the viewer's need to be closer to it diminishes his or her field of vision. With large objects, a greater distance is required to apprehend them as a whole, demanding the expansion of the viewer's field of vision.[4]

Which is to say, Minimalism's effort to expand the viewer's field of vision, which was equated with the expansion of the viewer's critical consciousness of the art-viewing experience, was predicated on certain formal strategies or interdictions that disallowed intimacy. For Morris, this entailed the 'maximum resistance to perceptual separation' and the evacuation of 'intimacy-producing relations'

Some/One 2001
Collection of the Samsung Museum of Modern Art, Seoul, Korea. Courtesy of Lehmann Maupin Gallery, New York

within the work, such as articulations of detail. His experiments with 'unitary' forms in the mid 1960s, which took 'relationships out of the work and [made] them a function of space, light, and the viewer's field of vision,' were based on the thesis that: 'Every internal relationship, whether it be set up by a structural division, a rich surface, or what have you, reduces the public, external quality of the object and tends to eliminate the viewer to the degree that these details pull him into an intimate relation with the work and out of the space in which the object exists.'[5]

One can argue, then, that as much as Suh's work extends the lessons of Minimalism, especially in mobilizing the viewer's body as a function of each of his installations, it also makes to varying degrees *anti*-minimalist moves in creating intimate relations with the viewer. Suh's work stages the public subject of Minimalism in terms of spatial orchestration, but negates it via the privacy of the details. Or, to use Morris' terms, it extends the viewer's field of vision then contracts or eliminates it. But these contradictions seem to afford certain reassurances to the viewers of Suh's work. For instance, consider the moment of discovery when you, as the viewer, come upon the semi-hidden details of *Floor* and *Who Am We?*. On the one hand, such moments are surprising in an *unnerving* way because you recognize that you were in the work before you knew it, that you were implicated or constituted as a public subject/body by the work before you became conscious of that fact. On the other hand, the moment is surprising in a *comforting* way because you uncovered a secret aspect of the work that explains it, resituating and restabilizing you as a private subject/body with a seemingly privileged access to the work's meaning. In other words, one aspect of Suh's work asserts decentred subjects and contingency of meaning; another aspect recentres the subject and provides interpretive closure. The satisfaction afforded by Suh's work is largely due to this doubleness. Each of his installations internally resolves for the viewer the potentially destabilizing conditions it initially proposes.

Take Two: Empty Collectivity

The scale of repetition and accumulation in much of Suh's work is impressive. While the individual elements – faces, figures, dog tags, and uniforms – remain more or less insignificant on their own, they overwhelm the viewer into a state of amazement, if not awe, when amassed into a collective image or object. As representations of identity and power, *Floor*, *Who Am We?*, *Some/One*, *High School Uni-Face* (1997), and *High School Uni-Form* each depicts the submission of individuals and their unique identities to a larger collective body in which the formal unity of the whole is dependent upon the uniformity and conformity of its parts. As models of individual subjects in relationship to collective social formations, be it a school, team, community, club, army, political party, or nation, Suh's work seems to assert that unity and belonging require sameness. After all, as his installations make obvious, one element out of place, one element of difference, jeopardizes the integrity of the whole.

This repression of individual difference and homogeneity of parts in many of Suh's projects is an ambiguous vision of human collectivity. It is unclear, for instance, whether the disciplined regularity of the jackets in *High School Uni-Form* or the more fluid yet highly controlled disposition of the dog tags in *Some/One* signals a critical view of disciplinary regimes of power or affirms the subjugation of individuals as a necessary precondition for the constitution of a collective identity. On the one hand, Suh's images of the renunciation of individualism resonate powerfully with traditional Korean/Eastern values, which consider self-sacrifice in the name of a larger social or political entity, like the family or a nation, to be a prime virtue. On the other hand, this virtuous submission of self to abstract notions of duty and honour is linked in Suh's work to the colonization of subjects and bodies. It is unclear whether order and discipline is imposed from the outside or regulated from within. The ambiguity also persists in *Floor*, which presents the 'masses' as the literal base of social space. Yet with the upturned hands of each of the small figures, it remains uncertain whether the work represents the resistant strength of the masses withstanding the weight of dominant power structures or their complicity in sustaining these structures. If *Floor* is in some sense a picture of contemporary society, it poses the question: Are we the agents of our liberation or of our oppression?

Suh's decision to divide *Floor* into the zone of the viewing bodies and the zone of the bodies viewed with a transparent material is highly suggestive. For, the glass floor that is also a glass ceiling provides visual continuity while at the same time enforcing a structural separation. As such, the work positions the viewer as both a dominat*ing* subject that is literally aligned with forces of power from above (stepping on the little people), and a dominat*ed* subject that is visually identified with the bodies of resistance/compliance below. This double positioning of the viewer is obviously intentional, and its legibility affords much pleasure for Suh's audience. Yet, the nature of this pleasure is questionable since it tends to override disturbing undercurrents in the work, such as repression of desire, internalization of discipline, and even implications of mass violence, sacrifice, and death. The sombre grandeur of *Some/One*, the gloomy memorializing of *High School Uni-Face*, and the ceremonial solemnity of *High School Uni-Form* all register the absence of masses of persons or bodies while exuding an aura of melancholic dignity.

Despite the numerous biographical explanations for such qualities in Suh's work, the dialectic between the individual and the collective is not simply an articulation of the artist's personal ambivalence.[6] It is more compelling, I think, to imagine Suh's work as approximating, responding to, and reflecting – probably unintentionally – the uncertain status of personal and collective identity in the broader context of the profound reorganization of cultural, social, economic, and political life described today as globalization. Michael Hardt and Antonio Negri's theorization of the new global order of 'Empire'

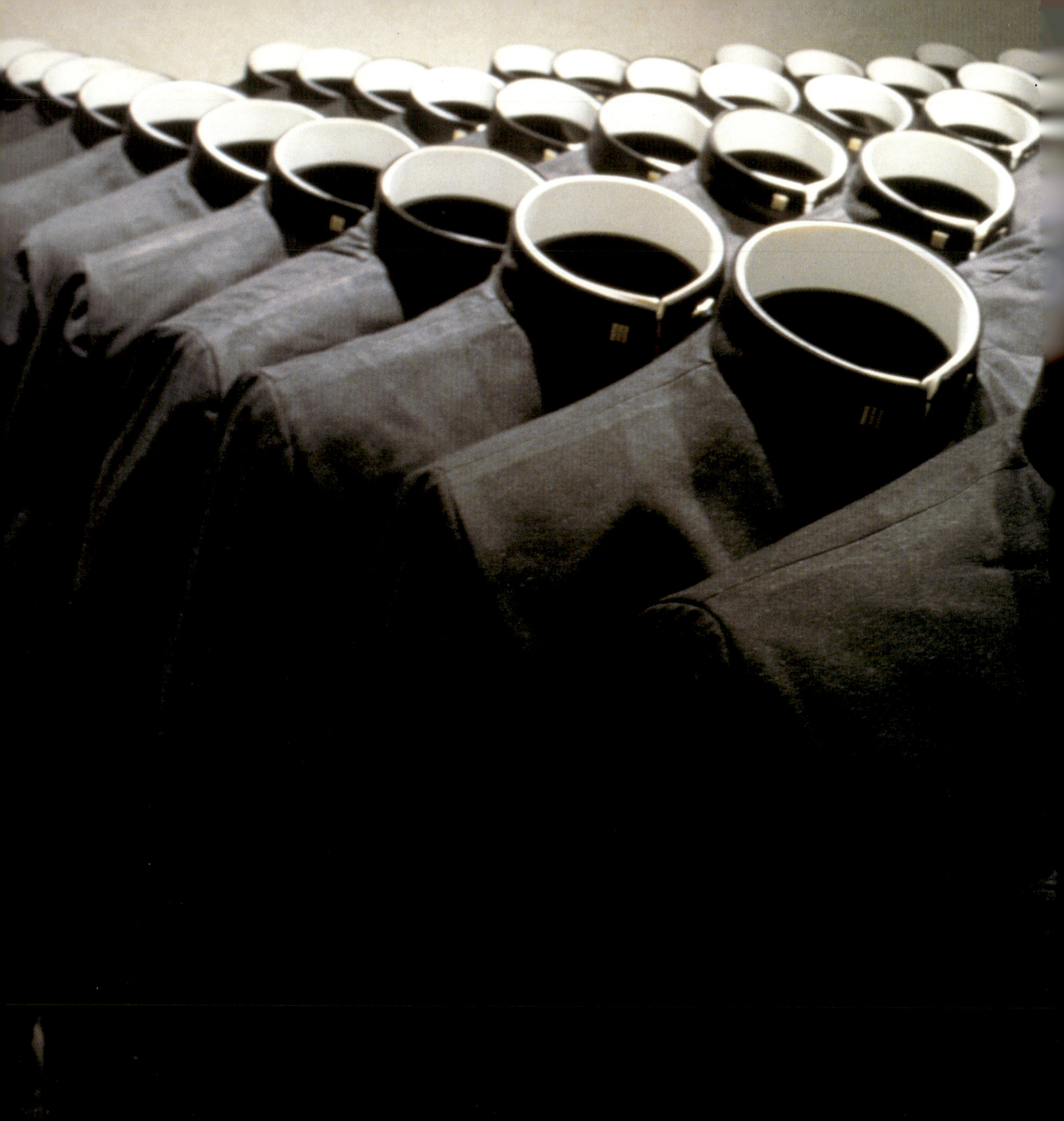

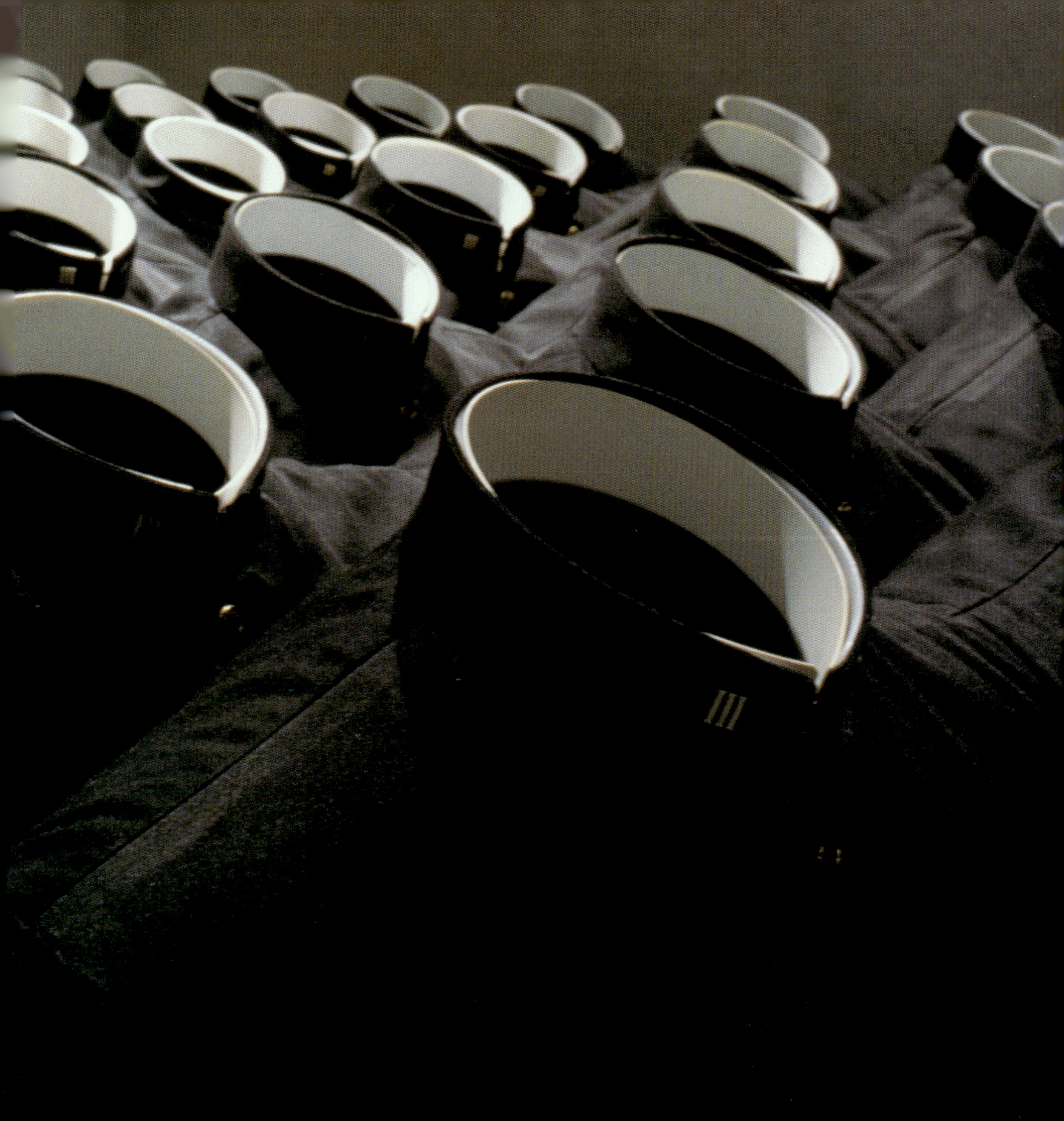

is particularly useful in this regard.[7] While it is inappropriate to rehearse the details of their extensive and controversial argument here, their proposition of 'the multitude' as a paradigm of subjectivity and collectivity that is distinct from 'the people' facilitates a more historical (rather than biographical) understanding of Suh's efforts.

In Hardt and Negri's thinking, the multitude is a figure of a new proletariat class that is constitutive of *and* resistant to the globally expanded reign of capitalist imperialism. Evolving out of the 'revolting masses' of the past, the multitude seeks liberation from the oppressive effects of imperialistic domination. Yet, unlike mass movements of the past, the multitude does not cohere as a unified collective body because it is not posed in opposition to a fixed figure of domination, such as a king or a nation-state. Mirroring the new logic of capitalism's power, which is unimpeded by geographical distance or boundaries, the multitude is conceived as temporary and inconclusive relations, a moving constellation of individual social agents.[8] According to Hardt and Negri, 'The multitude is a multiplicity, a plane of singularities, an open set of relations, which is not homogeneous or identical with itself and bears an indistinct, inclusive relation to those outside of it.'[9] Consequently, the shape of the multitude fluctuates over time according to particular, local necessities. The people, in contrast, 'is a constituted synthesis that is prepared for sovereignty… tend[ing] toward identity and homogeneity internally while posing its difference from and excluding what remains outside of it.'[10] As an assertion of a singular will and unified form, the people is aligned more with the historically waning era of the nation-state and less with the current post-nation conditions of globalization.

We can reconsider Suh's work given Hardt and Negri's paradigms. Is the collectivity represented in *Who Am We?*, *Floor*, *High School Uni-Form*, *High School Uni-Face*, and *Some/One* that of 'the multitude' or 'the people'? While *Who Am We?* leans towards the multitude with its lack of clear formal boundaries and seemingly limitless inclusiveness of persons without a unifying will or shared purpose, the other projects mentioned assert an overriding order. Suh's other works, even when they appear to do otherwise, resist the deterritorialized dispersal of subjects that the multitude implies, conjuring instead the coherence of the people. Invoking such unity and order at this particular historical moment is a retrogressive gesture, especially when the very terms of the constitution of identity – from individuals to nation-states – is being reformulated in light of and as part of a changing world order. Suh's representations of the people resonate with a range of twentieth-century images of the people, as varied as in the revolutionary aesthetics of Soviet photomontage, in the totalitarian aesthetics of social realism and fascism, and in the pluralist aesthetics of a democratic throng. And his reiteration of this model of the people's unity indicates a reluctance to concede an older fantasy of a collective body that functions as one.

Previous page: **High School Uni-Form** 1996
Collection David Teiger

But if Suh's work seems anachronistic in this regard, one should remember that his images of the people tend to be emptied out. Although *Some/One* appears heroic, it is a hollow shell propping up thousands of markers of absent, possibly lost, individuals. *High School Uni-Form*, similarly, conjures a ghostly assembly, as does *High School Uni-Face*. Even *Floor* is marked by pathos: all those people locked into one another, sustaining their collectivity, but for the mere purpose of resisting being crushed. The vacancy or absence at the core of Suh's rendering of collectivity mitigates the nostalgic desire to reclaim a triumphant model of the people and registers an elegiac recognition of its historical passing. This elegiac dimension distinguishes Suh's work from those of his contemporaries who address issues of identity under the pressures of globalization.

Take Three: Moving Spaces

Seoul Home... and *348 West 22nd St....*, are full-scale reproductions of Suh's two homes: the first in Korea where he grew up, the second in America where he currently resides. While both are constructed out of fabric and equally meticulous in their sewn detailing, *Seoul Home...*'s fluid silk in celadon green registers local and cultural specificity in a way that the unrefined and stiffer grey nylon of *348 West 22nd St....* does not, unless the local and cultural specificity of the New York abode is revealed precisely through its generic qualities. But if *Seoul Home...* is readily identifiable as belonging to a Korean cultural tradition, it has not been stuck in the land of its origination. *Seoul Home...* has travelled widely as its ever-growing title indicates. With the exhibitions at the Serpentine Gallery and the Seattle Art Museum, London and Seattle are officially added to its name. Likewise, *348 West 22nd St....* incorporates into its title the different venues around the world to which it travels. In fact, the titles of both pieces function as an itinerary that tracks each work's exhibition history, not unlike the accumulation of stamps from different countries in a passport. As such, even though the works replicate existing architectural structures in very specific locations, they are more about transience and mobility than permanence. The works are conceptualized as easily transportable homes, as spaces that can fit into a suitcase and be taken with you wherever you go.

There are at least two ways in which this mobilization of space, or, in Suh's words, the transportability and translatability of space, can be interpreted.[11] In the first instance, given that they are surrogate homes of the artist, these works can be viewed from a biographical perspective. Although Suh regularly travels back to his home in Korea, *Seoul Home...* is the site of his childhood past, charged with a nostalgic sentiment resulting from his move to the United States. It is now primarily a site of longing and memory. In contrast, *348 West 22nd St....* represents the artist's current living space, a displaced position in the United States against which *Seoul Home...* accrues greater emotional force as a lost origin. Hence, despite their separation in terms of geographical reference and their presentation as independent works, they are bound together as a continuous terrain of Suh's psychical and experiential reality.

In the second instance, the dualism in Suh's work – Korea as past, New York as present; Korea as projected site of longing and memory, New York as site of immediate reality – can be viewed as a more general commentary on the experience of cultural displacement. The dissimilar presentation strategies of *Seoul Home…* and *348 West 22nd St.…* further accentuate Suh's dualistic logic. The home of the past, longing, desire, and memory, with its transparent, weightless appearance and ethereal colour, hangs from the ceiling. *Seoul Home…* appears to be a ghostly apparition, something quite immaterial like an hallucination or a dream image. In this configuration, home is rendered unreal, and its space remains physically inaccessible to the viewers who gather beneath its delicate shadow, enraptured by its visually stunning presence. Unlike many of Suh's installations, *Seoul Home…* disallows an embodied experience of the work. The viewer can only see, not touch or enter, this diaphanous work, as if physical contact would break the spell of the perfection of home as a transcendent dream space.[12] Intentionally set in contrast is *348 West 22nd St.…*, which is grounded. With its ceiling suspended just enough to maintain the overall cubic shape and to articulate the interior volume of Suh's apartment, the work sits on the floor, emphasizing a sense of weight, collapsibility, and containment. The space of this home is continuous with the space of the viewer – 'more real', according to the artist – and it welcomes a comprehensive, embodied sensorial experience for the viewer who is allowed to enter its interior.[13]

The different presentations of these two works underline the clarity of Suh's dualistic vision. But the segregation of what is a 'real' and what is an imagined space/home has other effects, too. For example, the physical elevation of *Seoul Home…* to a height above the heads and out of reach of its viewers not only reifies the space, it objectifies the work and 'elevates' it as a precious object of pure aesthetic contemplation. The otherworldliness of *Seoul Home…* becomes a new kind of idealism, disconnected from the materiality of social conditions that constitute the basis of even our dreams. *348 West 22nd St.…* is not idealized or 'elevated' in the same way as *Seoul Home…* in so far as it shares the same 'real' space as that of the viewer. But in conjuring an all-enveloping simulacral environment, it too obscures the conditions of its being by becoming its own context.

When the artist connects *Seoul Home…* and *348 West 22nd St.…*, the division between the realms of reality/present and longing/past will hopefully become blurred.[14] Conjoined as a single piece, in what could be viewed as a utopian gesture, the work may better articulate the complex ways in which reality and desire, past and present mutually contaminate each other. 'Reality' is already a product of desire, and desire is inextricably, if eccentrically, tied to 'real' circumstances. Similarly, the experiential elasticity of time – its acceleration, deceleration, reversal, overlap, suspension, etc. – which confounds the rational view of time as an homogeneous material with a regulated and unidirectional flow, may also be better represented when *Seoul Home…* and *348 West 22nd St.…* are joined.

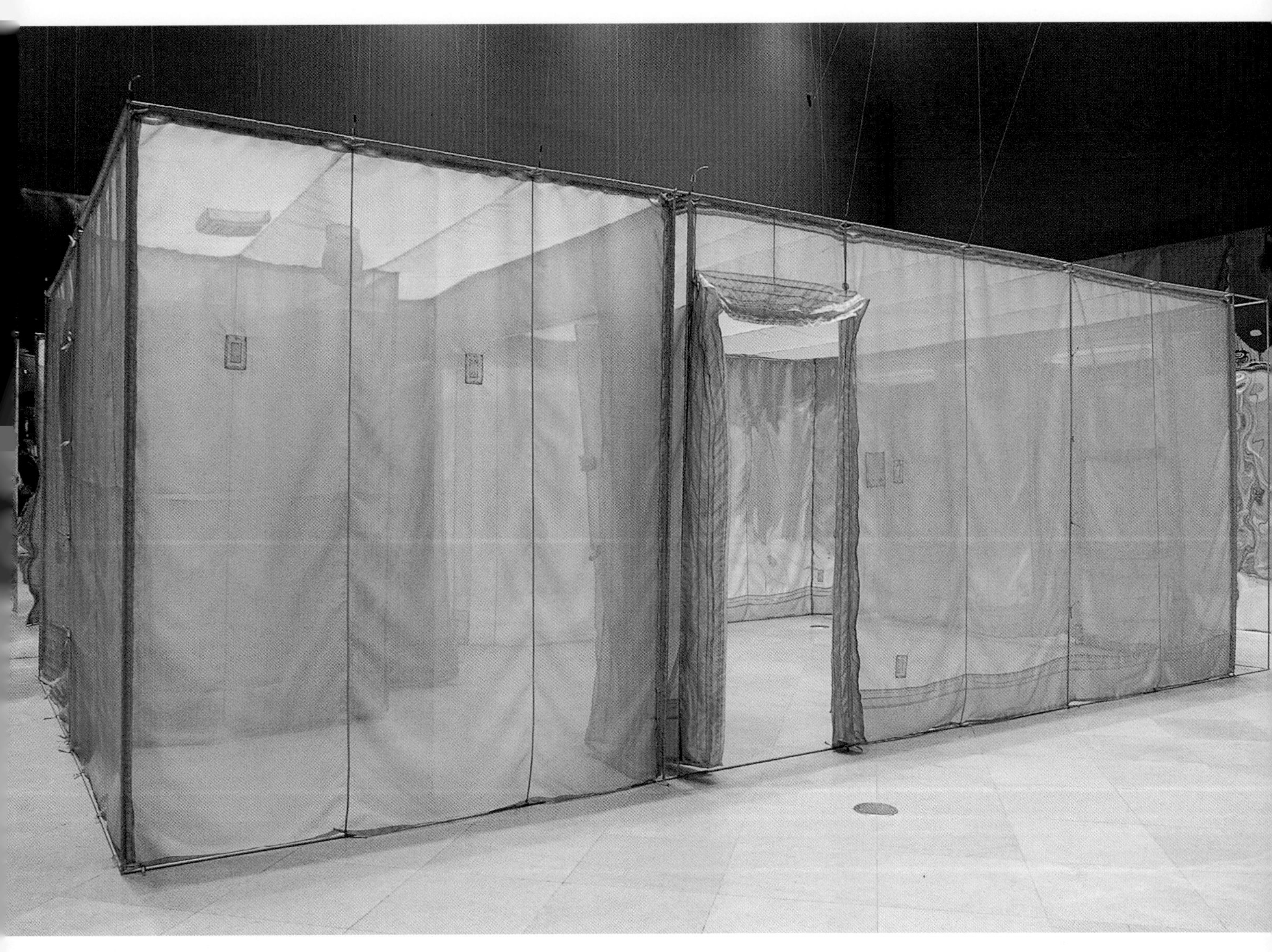

348 West 22nd St., Apt. A, New York, NY 10011 at Rodin Gallery, Seoul/Tokyo Opera City Art Gallery/ Serpentine Gallery, London/Biennale of Sydney/Seattle Art Museum 2000
Installation view at Rodin Gallery, Seoul. Collection Ninah and Michael Lynne

However, this will not mitigate the ways in which these two works assert a new sense of artistic autonomy. Despite the dependence on the architecture of given exhibition sites, *Seoul Home…* and *348 West 22nd St.…* maintain a self-sufficiency that complicates the premise of site-specific art, as something physically bound to a particular location, thus immovable. Suh has stated: 'By making highly movable site-specific installations, I question the concept not only of specificity but also of the site itself implied within the notion of site-specificity.'[15] Yet, even as transportability is proposed in *Seoul Home…* and *348 West 22nd St.…* as a critique of the conventional notion of site-specific art, it simultaneously leads to what looks like the return of the autonomy of the artwork. Or, because these works are traces of specific architectural spaces, carrying around their own contexts from place to place, they function quite literally as worlds unto themselves.

In her 1977 essay, 'Notes on the Index: Seventies Art in America', Rosalind Krauss theorized that what we now call site-specific art is fundamentally indexical in nature: it is an imprint or trace rather than a mimetic semblance of a referential presence.[16] She argued that art produced in immediate response to or as a direct physical trace of the existing conditions of a site disavows autonomous 'inner' meaning. Leaning on Roland Barthes' writings, she likened such context-dependent art to a photograph, as 'a message without a code', whose meaning is open and vulnerable to the fluctuating contingencies of its context. Stretching the photographic analogy further, she argued that site-specific art renders its architectural surroundings into a 'caption', and that rather than calling attention to itself as the source of meaning, site-specific art deflects it towards the site. The self-sufficiency of *Seoul Home…* and *348 West 22nd St.…* contradicts Krauss' thesis. This is in part because Krauss focused primarily on indexicality as a mode of artistic production that reorganizes the construction of meaning; she did not fully explore the ramifications of the *circulation* of such production. Granted, the question of 'movable site-specific installations' was not on the horizon in the 1970s as it is today. But the link Krauss draws between site-specific art and the photograph opens up ways of thinking about the possibilities and pitfalls of the widespread mobilization of site-specificity in contemporary art, of which Suh's work is an example.[17]

Clearly, Suh's *Seoul Home…* and *348 West 22nd St.…* are products of indexical procedures. Like a photograph, they meticulously and exactingly replicate a referential presence – the domestic spaces of the artist's two homes – in order that this presence may materialize in other locations and other contexts as a trace, as a marker of an absent presence. But unlike a photograph, the meaning of *Seoul Home…* or *348 West 22nd St.…* is self-contained and not easily given to redirection; it remains intact no matter where it is installed. Are the London and Seattle installations of *Seoul Home…* and *348 West 22nd St.…* fundamentally different to the prior versions in New York or Los Angeles? Does the status of the original sites that these works represent change from city to city? Suh's practice would seem to teach us that in the very moment of transporting site specificity, indexical procedures

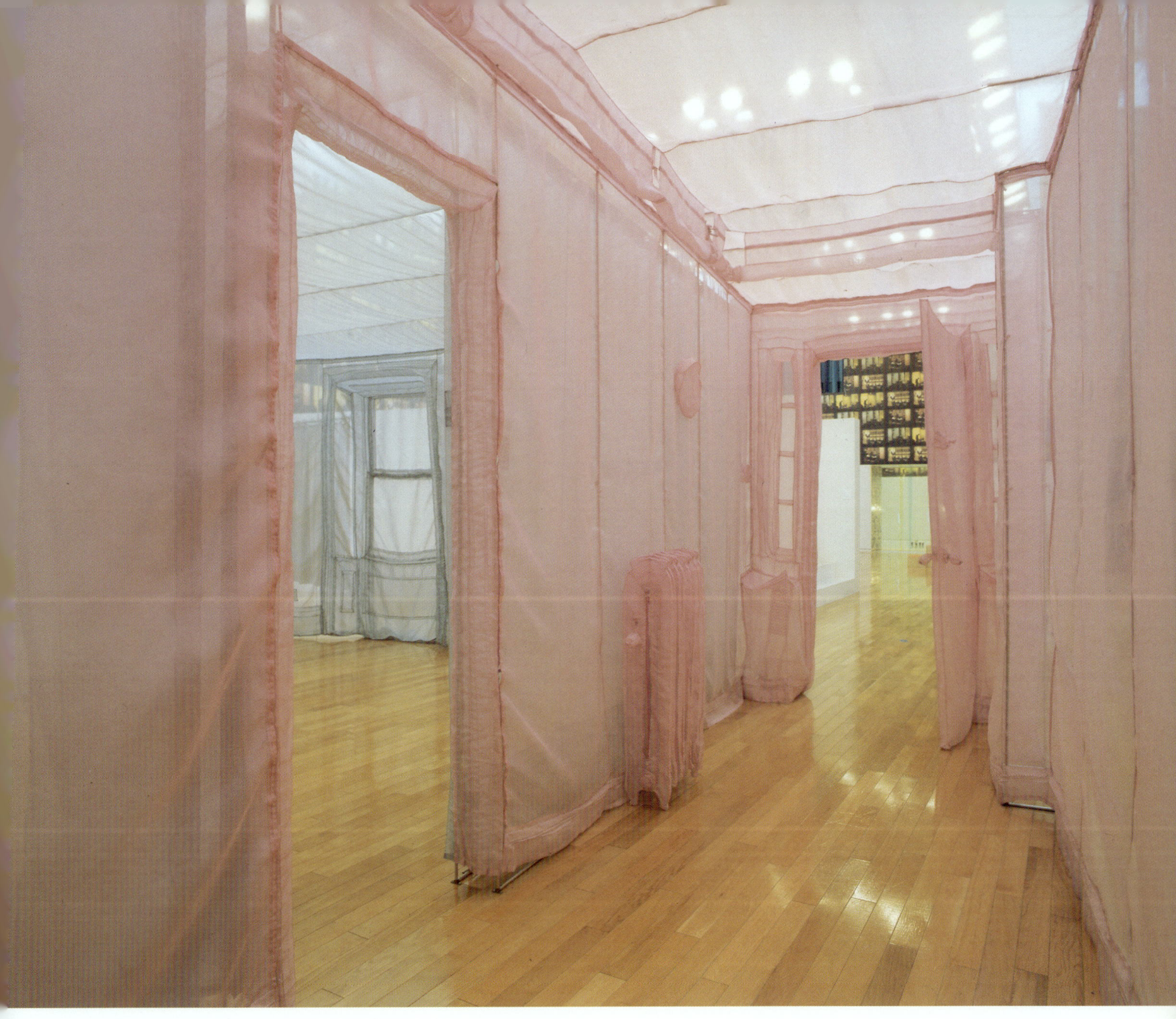

348 West 22nd St., Apt. A, New York, NY 10011 at Rodin Gallery, Seoul/Tokyo Opera City Art Gallery/ Serpentine Gallery, London/Biennale of Sydney/Seattle Art Museum (corridor) 2001
Courtesy of the artist and Lehmann Maupin Gallery, New York

become iconic images, or simply sculpture in a more traditional sense. The fact of the mobility of *Seoul Home...* and *348 West 22nd St....* is nominally registered, of course, in the ongoing extension of the works' respective titles. But the actualities of travel and the particularities of various other exhibition locations and contexts leave no trace on the works' form or their meaning. The lesson to be drawn from this is that in order for the binding of transportability and site specificity to work as a critique, itinerancy itself needs to be *indexically* registered.

•

In a recent *Artforum* article on Do-Ho Suh's work, critic Frances Richard writes of *Seoul Home...*: 'Premised in autobiography yet dematerialized to a lyrical husk, *Seoul Home...* appears as a scrim onto which anybody may project his or her reveries about any absent home.'[18] The timing of this remark, which is representative of the general critical reception of *Seoul Home...*, is extremely interesting. How is it that in 2002 *anyone*, presumably no matter what their cultural background or gender, can equally project personal fantasies or dreams about *any* absent home onto a work that is so unambiguously Asian, and uncommon even in the tradition of Korean domestic architecture?[19] It does not seem too long ago that the celebration and criticism (in the media, market, and institutions alike) of works like *Seoul Home...* was predicated on the legibility of the signs of its cultural difference. In the 1990s during the debates surrounding multiculturalism and identity politics, the attention that mainstream institutions gave to work produced by non-Western artists seemed to be in direct proportion to the obviousness of its 'otherness'. What has happened since then that the signs of otherness are no longer recognized as such and perceived instead as signs of a universal experience?

Today, in the context of a more globalized media and market system, it seems that a greater variety of signs of cultural difference are gaining broader public attention. This is a welcome shift in so far as the playing field of contemporary art is extending across the world, with non-Western and (ex-) Third World countries emerging as vital nodes of contemporary art activity and exchange. New 'centres' have emerged, such as Johannesburg, Havanna, Sydney, Kwang-Ju, among many others, to relativize the longstanding centrality of cities such as New York, Paris and London. And audiences of contemporary art are learning new visual vocabularies and histories to take in the expanded range of works on view. However, the apparent geographical decentralization of the art network, with presumptions of equalization of resources, access and distribution across a more expanded terrain of operation, obscures the global consolidation of certain cultural values that align with existing hierarchies of relations among different nations, corporations, institutions and economies. (This is in part why so many of the same artists and curators participate in the staging of international 'mega-exhibitions', and why so many of these exhibitions look and feel the same.) Within the context of this expanded and consolidated art network, signs of cultural difference, both in terms of the artwork and the artist, are espoused by the art media, market, and institutions for reasons quite contrary to those of a mere ten years ago.

What so many critics, including Frances Richard, appreciate most in Suh's *Seoul Home...* are not the particularities of its architectural style, ornamental details, type of sewing, and type of fabric, which all signify 'Korea', or at least 'Asia'.[20] In fact, these qualities of otherness are repressed as secondary. Critics and audiences see *through* the signs of cultural specificity and (mis)recognize a commonality of itinerancy. The work is seen as commentary on or an analogue for the destabilized but pervasive conditions of nomadism, migration, and cosmopolitan homelessness, acknowledged as a new universal by and for those of a particular cultural, professional, and economic class.[21] Ironically, it is precisely because Suh's work can be identified with an Asian or Korean cultural source, and because the artist himself is a culturally displaced subject from Korea, that it garners accolades in the international art context. What is truly valued in Suh's work is not its authenticity as a product of another culture but its capacity to register through that authenticity *another* authenticity of itinerancy and cultural displacement. Even the spectacularized labour of the meticulous sewing, the overwhelmingly impressive assertion of the handmade in *Seoul Home...* and *High School Uni-Form* is a coded sign of otherness that elliptically conjures the cultures of women, domesticity, and the sweatshop (which is resonant of Asian women's labour in particular).

The ascendance of an artist like Do-Ho Suh in the international art scene is not only predicated on the high quality of workmanship, cleverness of ideas, strength and clarity of formal decisions, and sophistication of talent. It is also linked to the fact that in the contemporary art world today, a culturally displaced person of adequate means who can navigate a bigger map of the world than those bound to one location, culture, or identity is treated as a representative if not privileged person, able to speak to, speak of, and speak as a retooled nomadic subject of globalization. Suh's recurring trips to Korea, motivated in large measure by the necessities of his production (labour is cheaper there), also mirrors the ongoing uneven distribution of labour, resources, and power in late capitalism. Thus, the attraction that Suh's work draws from a globalized art network of curators, dealers, collectors, and critics lies in the symbiotic fashioning of both the work and the artist within the logic of a new order of mobilized identities. Do-Ho Suh's art eulogizes the older paradigms of subjectivity, identity and space while announcing new versions of them as unlocated conditions of transience.

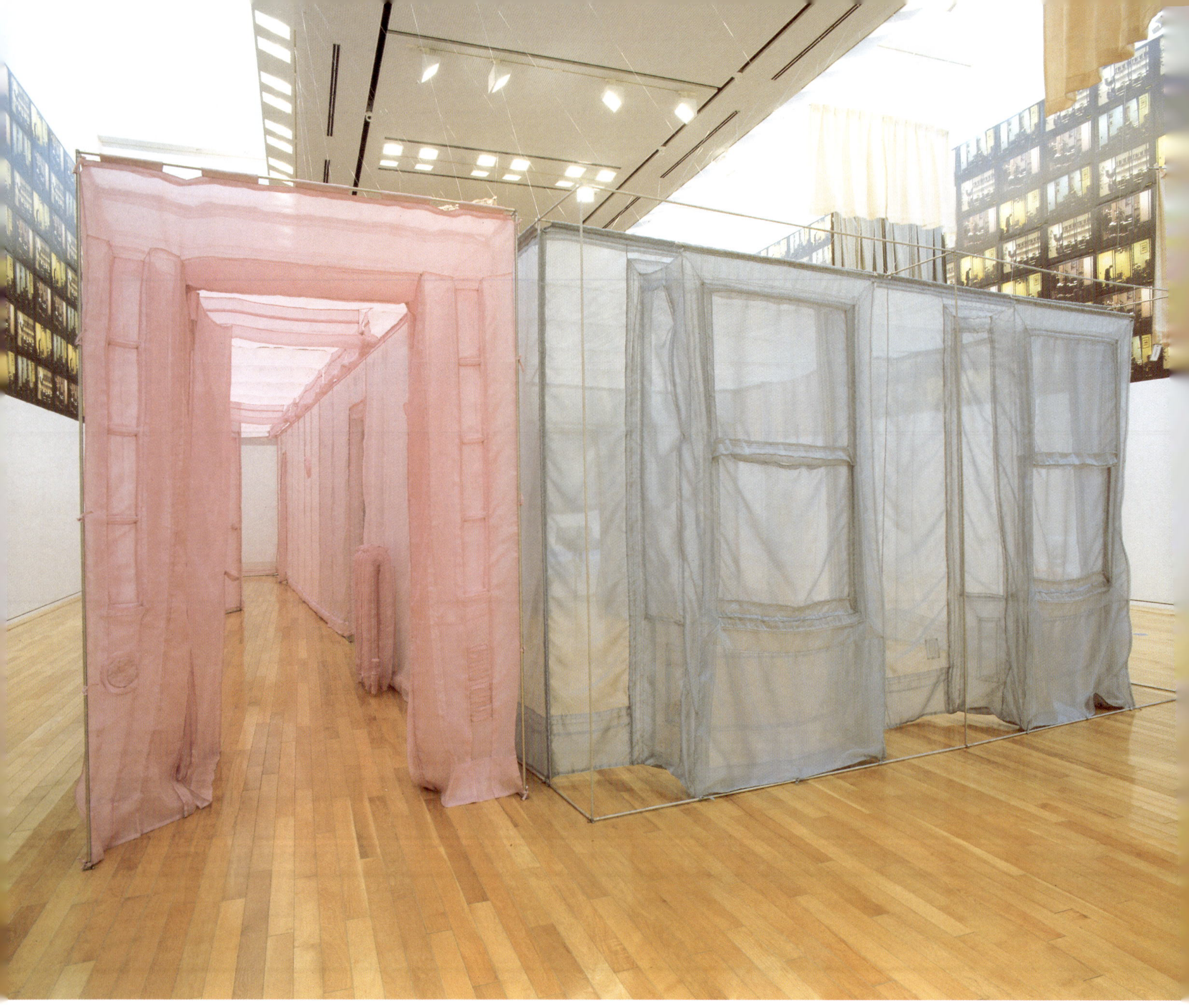

348 West 22nd St., Apt. A, New York, NY 10011 at Rodin Gallery, Seoul/Tokyo Opera City Art Gallery/ Serpentine Gallery, London/Biennale of Sydney/Seattle Art Museum 2000 and **348 West 22nd St., Apt. A, New York, NY 10011 at Rodin Gallery, Seoul/Tokyo Opera City Art Gallery/Serpentine Gallery, London/ Biennale of Sydney/Seattle Art Museum (corridor)** 2001
Courtesy of the artist and Lehmann Maupin Gallery, New York

Footnotes

1 Janet Kraynak, 'Traveling in Do-Ho Suh's World', *La Biennale di Venezia/ Korean Pavilion, Do-Ho Suh*, exh. cat. (Seoul: The Korean Culture and Arts Foundation): 41–2. See also Miwon Kwon, 'Uniform Appearance', *frieze* (February 1998). In 2001, *Seoul Home...* was included in the *BodySpace* exhibition at the Baltimore Museum of Art (curated by Helen Molesworth), which specifically featured works by a younger generation of artists extending the terms of Minimalism.

2 Critic Clement Greenberg's theory of modernist art, which espoused the autonomy of art and specificity of medium, dominated the art discourse of the decades following World War II in the United States. His call for a self-referential rather than contextual approach to artistic production and aesthetic experience came under attack by the subsequent generation of artists in the 1960s. For a critique of the complex relationship between Greenbergian modernism and Minimalism, see Hal Foster, 'The Crux of Minimalism' in *The Return of the Real* (Cambridge: MIT Press, 1996).

3 This is to contradict Frank Stella's famous dictum regarding the logic of his Minimalist paintings: 'What you see is what you see.'

4 In Morris' words: 'It is necessary literally to keep one's distance from large objects in order to take the whole of any one view into one's field of vision. The smaller the object the closer one approaches it and, therefore, it has correspondingly less of a spatial field in which to exist for the viewer. It is this necessary greater distance of the object in space from our bodies, in order that it be seen at all, that structures the non-personal or public mode.' See Robert Morris, 'Notes on Sculpture, Part II', *Artforum* (October 1966): 20–3.

5 Ibid.

6 Typical of such a biographical interpretation is Katie Clifford, 'A Soldier's Story', *Art News* (January 2002): 102–5. Clifford attributes the imagery, material, and organization of works such as *High-School Uni-Form* and *Some/One* to the artist's three-year mandatory service in the Korean army. Similarly, Clifford interprets Suh's fabric architecture projects as a kind of expressionism, that is, as a reflection of the artist's personal experience of cultural displacement, rather than as a reflection of broader socioeconomic and historical conditions.

7 See Michael Hardt and Antonio Negri, *Empire* (Cambridge: Harvard University Press, 2000).

8 Paradoxically, the multitude also facilitates the system's ongoing prosperity even as it threatens to destroy it. The multitude is constitutive of and resistant to, productive and destructive of Empire, which contradictively liberates and oppresses human desire. Ibid.: 60–1.

9 Ibid.: 103.

10 Ibid.

11 Undated artist statement, *c.*1997.

12 The withdrawal of the work from viewers by hanging it from the ceiling is also instigated by the artist's desire to protect the work from physical damage. In its premiere exhibition at the Korean Cultural Center in Los Angeles, the work was suspended over a stairway in such a way that viewers walked up into the work and out through one of its door openings. There was no vantage point from which to take in the entirety of the work in one view.

13 E-mail communication with author, 23 February 2002.

14 Such a plan is in preparation for an exhibition of Suh's work at the Kemper Contemporary Art Museum in Kansas City in December 2002. For this show, the artist is producing a new version of *Seoul Home...* in ivory silk with red thread, to be connected to *348 West 22nd St....*

15 Undated artist statement, *c.* 1997.

16 Rosalind Krauss, 'Notes on the Index: Seventies Art in America', *October* 3 (1977): 16–32; reprinted as 'Notes on the Index Part 2' in *The Originality of the Avant-Garde and Other Modernist Myths* (Cambridge: MIT Press, 1985): 196–219. The works that Krauss refers to are from the *Rooms* exhibition held at P.S.1, including works by Gordon Matta-Clark, Michelle Stuart, and Lucio Pozzi, among others.

17 See Miwon Kwon, *One Place After Another: Site-Specific Art and Locational Identity* (Cambridge: MIT Press, 2002) on these and related issues concerning site specificity.

18 Frances Richard, 'Home in the World', *Artforum* (January 2002): 115.

19 *Seoul Home...* is not a typical Korean house. It is a replica of a replica of a replica. The house that Suh renders in fabric is of his father's reconstruction of a nineteenth-century building from a secret garden of the king's palace. The artist's father salvaged the timber from its demolition during the 1960s. The original building was itself designed to mimic a commoner's home so that the king could, on occasion, find reprieve from the formality of his royal abode and get closer to his people without venturing outside the palace complex. It also charges Suh's work with a certain Oedipal tension.

20 The special type of traditional Korean stitching used on this project is reserved for the handling of extremely delicate fabrics that have a tendency to sag and stretch, such as the green silk used in *Seoul Home...* To prevent the unravelling of the fabric and to stabilize it, the seams are sewn from the front and back sides so that in the finished state inside and outside are hardly distinguishable. This equivalence in the case of *Seoul Home...* also functions metaphorically as the blurring of the boundaries between interior and exterior spaces. The silk itself is quite identifiable to Korea, not only in terms of colour and quality but also in terms of the particularly narrow width that it comes in.

21 See Kraynak, op cit.

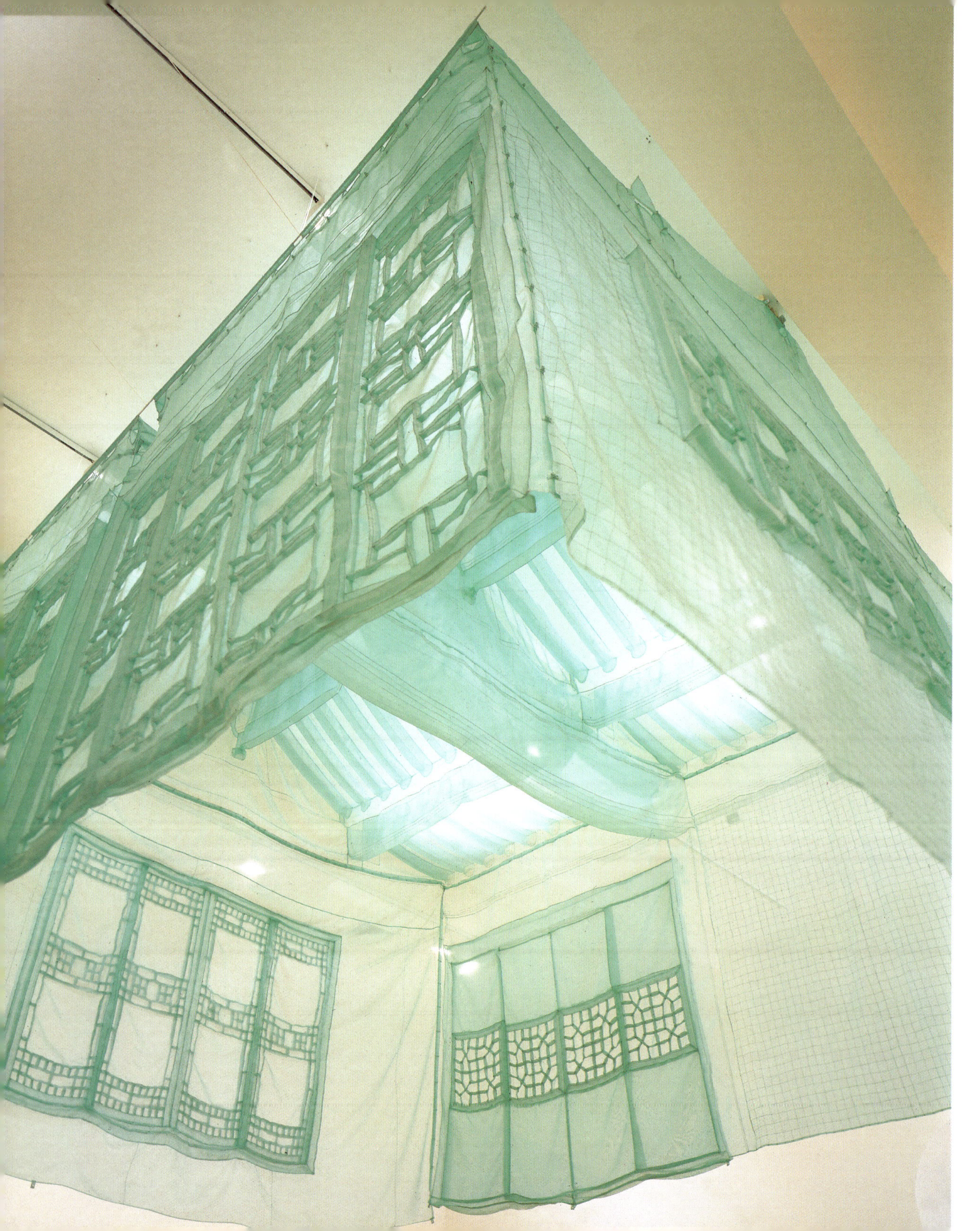

The Perfect Home: A Conversation with Do-Ho Suh

Lisa G. Corrin

The Perfect Home is an evolving series of related sculptural installations fabricated of diaphanous fabric in celadon green, pink and blue-grey and 'patterned' after the architecture of Suh's childhood home in Seoul and his apartment in New York. Conceived individually as 'custom-made clothing for a room', together they represent the most complete statement to date of Suh's ongoing investigation of 'transportable site-specificity', his term for the nomadic character of works of art whose meaning migrates with their presentation in different contexts. Intended as a way to consider notions of displacement, each piece relocates a space that is filled with the artist's personal associations to the context of the art gallery, transferring private references to the public domain.

Suh began making sculpture associated with architecture when he was a fine art student at the Rhode Island School of Design, from which he graduated in 1994. As part of his course work he chose to take classes in pattern-making, a skill that ultimately enabled him to realize a number of sculptural interventions in corridors and inconspicuous passageways, places on the periphery of inhabited spaces. According to the artist, these exercises in dislocation deliberately disoriented the viewer and were an early attempt to find a meaningful gesture through which to highlight the character of overlooked spaces and their impact on human interaction. In 1999, he was commissioned to create an installation for the Korean Cultural Center in Los Angeles. The resulting piece, *Seoul Home/L.A. Home*, introduced specific cultural references into his architectural works. It also marked the starting point for the creation of pieces that explore nostalgic evocations of 'home' by connecting his country of origin to his new surroundings in the United States.

Born in Seoul, South Korea in 1962, Do-Ho Suh is the son of the distinguished Korean artist and scholar Se-Ok Suh, renowned for his large-scale ink paintings linking traditional calligraphy with modern brush painting. His mother, Min-Za Chung, is one of the founders of Arumjigi-Culture Keepers, a group devoted to preserving the disappearing traditions and heritage of Korea. The family home in Seoul where Suh grew up is a complex of five contemporary and traditional structures, one of which is built of the red-pine timbers from a nineteenth-century building originally located in the grounds of the royal palace.[1] It is within this cultural landscape that Suh's artistic formation has coalesced. The following conversation took place in December 2001, and explores the development and production of *The Perfect Home* and its sources in traditional Korean architecture.

Seoul Home/L.A. Home/New York Home/Baltimore Home/London Home/Seattle Home 1999
Installation view at P.S.1 Contemporary Art Center, Long Island City
The Museum of Contemporary Art, Los Angeles. Purchased with funds provided by an Anonymous donor and a gift of the artist

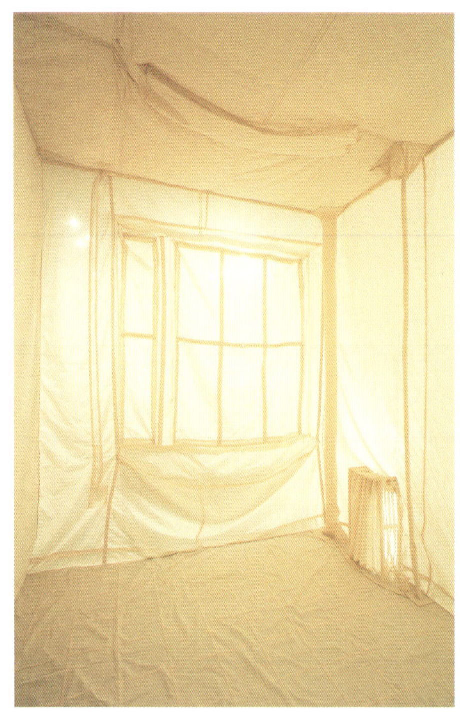

Room 516-II 1994
Installation view at Columbia University, New York
Courtesy of the artist and Lehmann Maupin Gallery, New York

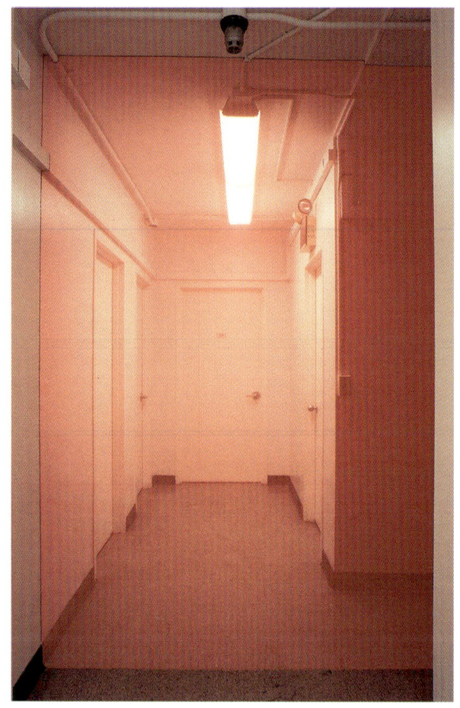

Red Conjunction 1995
Installation view at Columbia University, New York
Courtesy of the artist and Lehmann Maupin Gallery, New York

Lisa G. Corrin What was the starting point for the idea of making 'clothing for spaces'?

Do-Ho Suh Before I went to graduate school at Yale, where I got an M.F.A. in sculpture in 1997, I was living in an apartment in New York across the street from a fire station. It was very noisy, and I couldn't really sleep. I was thinking at the time, 'Gosh, when was the last time I had a really good sleep?' and I remembered my old room back in my childhood home in Korea. Then I started thinking about how I could bring my old room into the space of my new apartment. That is when I came up with the idea of a fabric room.

LC How did you do it? What was the context for the piece?

D-HS In 1994, I wanted to find out the feasibility of producing a large-scale fabric house, so I tried it first on a small scale. The piece, *Room 516/516-I/516-II* (1994), was created by covering my studio space in muslin. Fortunately, it worked.

However, I did not have a chance to realize the Korean house project until I was invited to do a project at the Korean Cultural Center in L.A. in 1999. In the centre of that space there is a huge spiral staircase about 20-feet wide. I became interested in that space. On the first floor I saw a

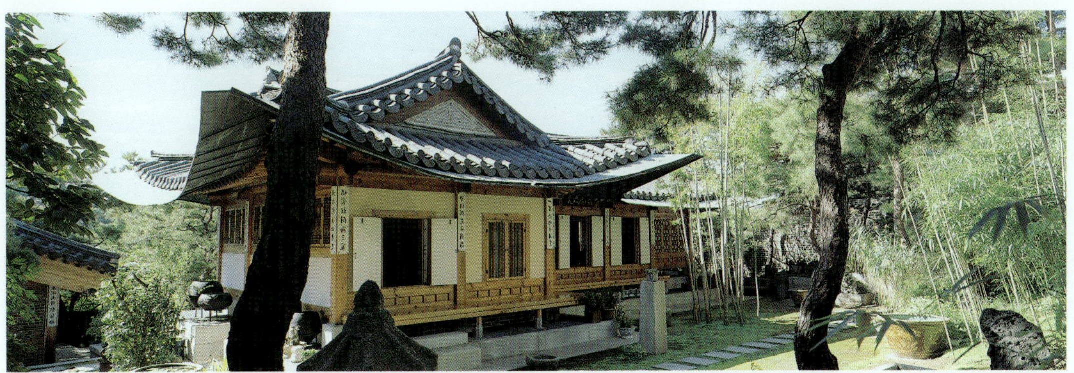

The house of Do-Ho Suh's parents, Min-Za Chung and Se-Ok Suh

corner with displays about traditional Korean architecture. In one of those displays was a photograph of a nineteenth-century building that reminded me of my family home. The photograph depicted an unusual building in the palace complex in Seoul that had a similar function to the 'cottage' to which Marie Antoinette sometimes escaped within the grounds of Versailles. King Sunjo, the twenty-third sovereign of the Yi Dynasty, wanted to experience the life of ordinary people. In 1828, he ordered a civilian-style house to be built in the secret garden of the palace complex. Only members of the royal family were allowed to see it. Ironically, that building is considered one of the most beautiful examples of Korean traditional architecture. One-hundred-and-fifty years later, in the 1970s, my father 'modelled' a building for our family after the royal home pictured in the photograph, not the entire complex, but just the master's quarters and the library.

During the 1950s and 60s, a lot of the palace complex had to be dismantled because the roads were being widened. The two-hundred-year-old lumber used for those buildings was sold as firewood. My father collected this lumber over a period of many years and used it in the design for the house where I grew up. It was an exact duplicate of the original civilian-style house in the palace grounds. Ironically, the original materials used to build the palace were reused to construct its duplicate. In another twist of fate, the duplicate created by my father is now being used as a model for the redecoration of the original house.

LC Your piece, *Seoul Home/L.A. Home/New York Home/Baltimore Home/London Home/ Seattle Home* adds another layer of meaning to the story. It is another step further removed from the original, capturing only its simplified form and traces of its details. Its shape, one might say, is that of memory. Your memories of your family home must have remained very vivid. Did you ever see the building upon which your father's duplicate was based?

D-HS I still remember clearly the late afternoon one May when my parents took me to the original house. I was in the fourth grade. There was no-one except my family and two engineers present.

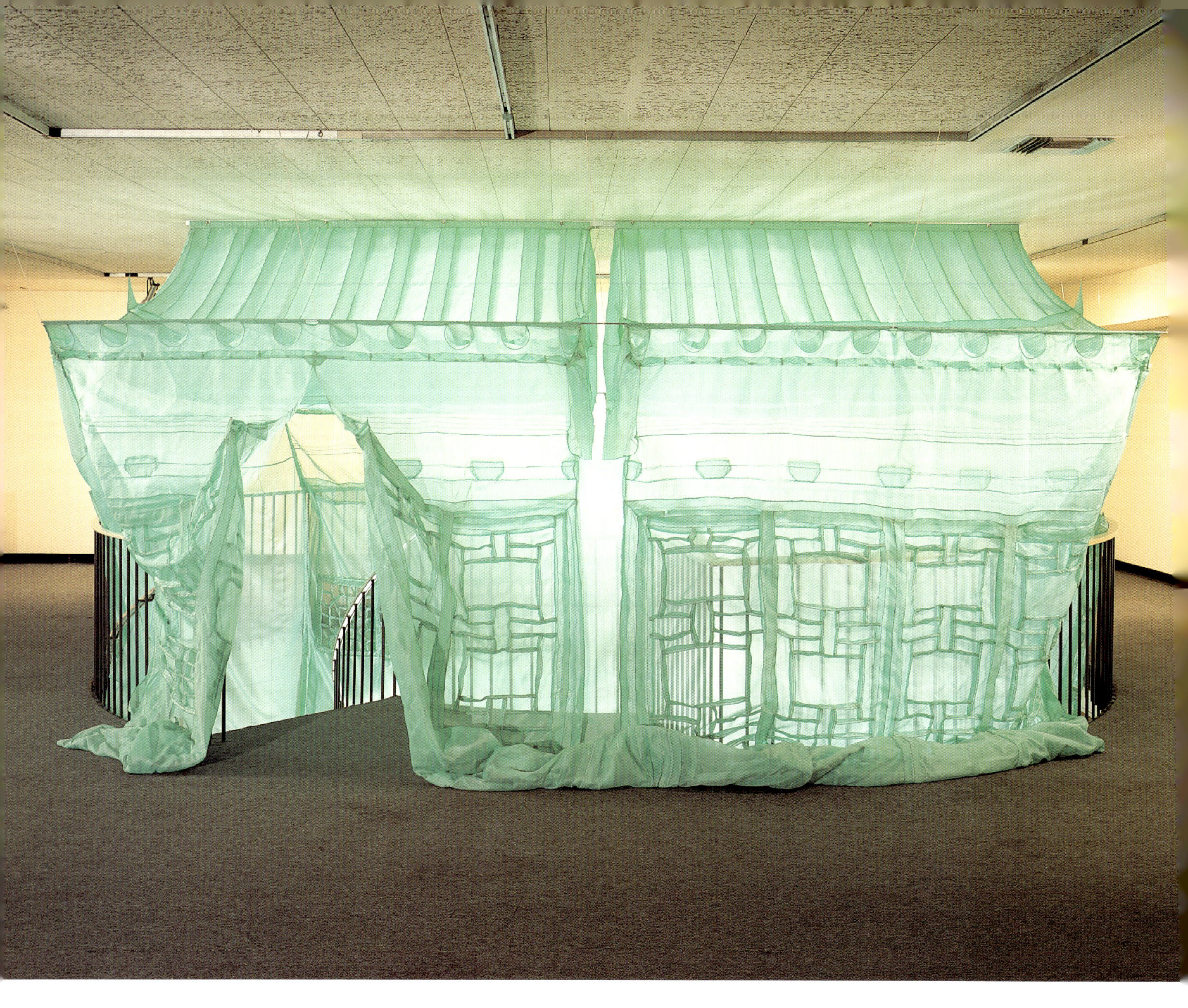

Seoul Home/L.A. Home/New York Home/Baltimore Home/London Home/Seattle Home 1999
Installation view at the Korean Cultural Center, Los Angeles
The Museum of Contemporary Art, Los Angeles. Purchased with funds provided by an Anonymous donor and a gift of the artist

We had to get special permits to go into the house to measure the building. We measured all afternoon and talked about the experience the rest of the day. I haven't been there since. I intend to go back this spring.

LC So, the Korean Cultural Center presented a unique context for your work to connect to this early experience of traditional Korean architecture?

D-HS Yes, I wanted to bring that one-room house to the space. I made the piece using the house in Korea as a template, then took it down, folded it, packed it in my suitcase and brought it to L.A. It was suspended from the ceiling of the second floor and hung down over the staircase. The staircase was the only way to access the second floor of the Center so everyone who came had to literally walk into the piece and experience it physically. As viewers walked around the second floor, they had a weird view of the house. They were able to look down upon the same space they had just walked in and through.

LC Did the piece become a transitional space within the context of the Korean Cultural Center? Did that idea come from working with hallways in your early hallway pieces?

D-HS On a subconscious level I must have continued to think about passageways. They connected to my personal experience of being physically transported from Korea to the United States. The Korean Cultural Center is a space of cultural displacement. It transports, introduces and installs Korean culture within a foreign context. The first floor is used to display some Korean archeological artifacts and objects related to traditional folk culture. The second floor is where contemporary Korean art and works by Korean American artists in the Los Angeles area are shown. It is like a passageway establishing the close proximity and yet the immense gap between nostalgia for the 'native' culture of the past and the immigrant culture of the present. The architectural element of the staircase not only separates but also connects these two spaces and time periods.

LC The title of the piece reinforces the metaphor of cultural displacement.

D-HS It is called *Seoul Home/L.A. Home/New York Home/Baltimore Home/London Home/Seattle Home*. When the piece was made, it was *Seoul Home* and when I transported it to Los Angeles it became *Seoul Home/L.A. Home*. Every time I show the piece in a different city, the name of the city becomes part of the title. So far, I have shown the piece in Baltimore and New York, and now the title will also include the cities of London and Seattle. With each installation in a different city or country, the piece acquires new dimensions, literally and figuratively. I want the piece to bear the trace of each of these passages and the 'residences' it experiences. As the ongoing readjustment of the title demonstrates, my project expands the notion of home with each installation in a new space.

LC *Seoul Home...* is part of a series of related pieces. Can you describe the evolution of the work based on your New York apartment?

D-HS I was invited to participate in *My Home is Yours. Your Home is Mine.* at the Rodin Gallery in Seoul (2000). The exhibition focused on nomadism and the idea of 'home'. It was very interesting to me because, by then, I was living in New York. I decided to bring my New York space – my

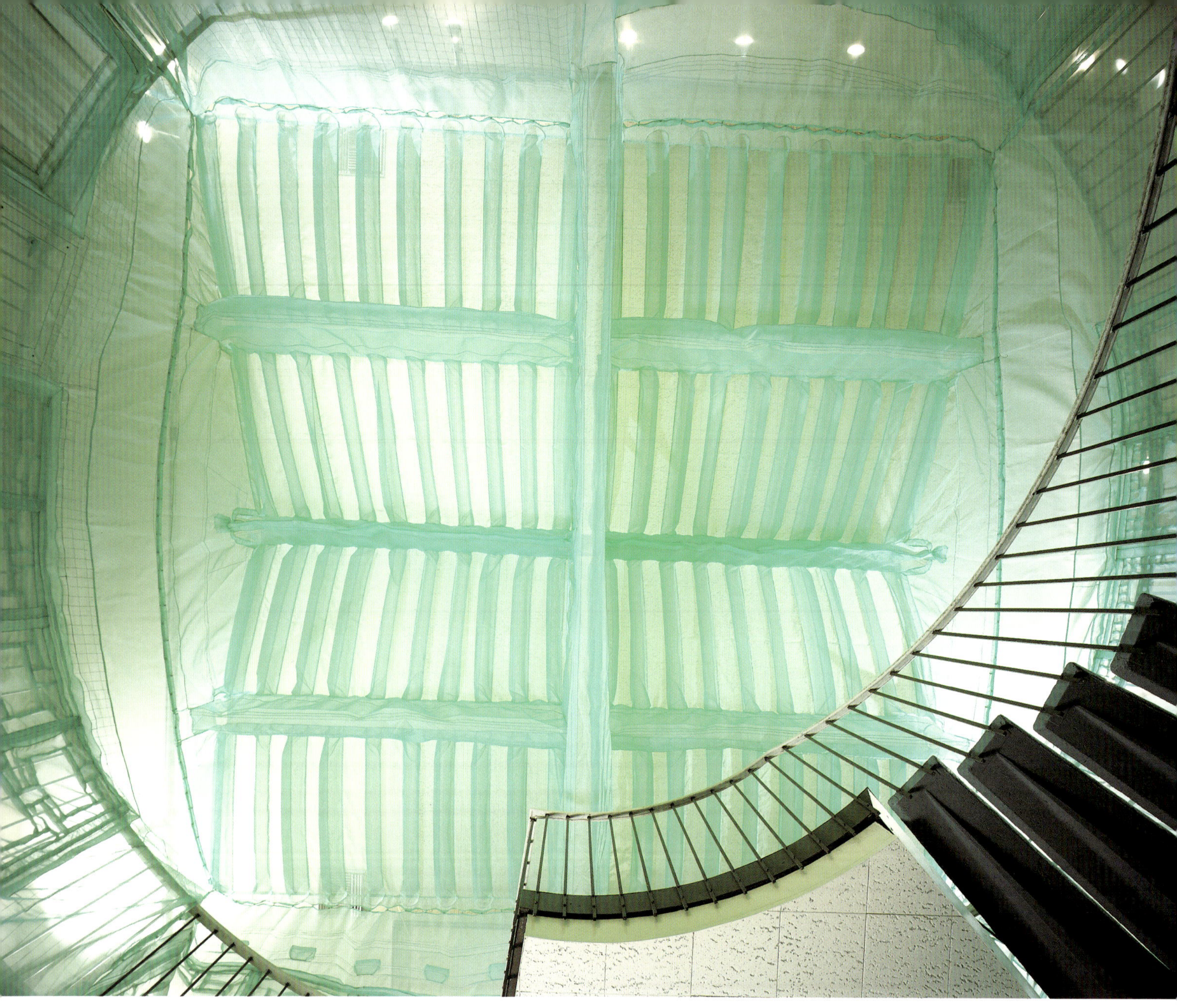

Seoul Home/L.A. Home/New York Home/Baltimore Home/London Home/Seattle Home 1999
Installation view at the Korean Cultural Center, Los Angeles
The Museum of Contemporary Art, Los Angeles. Purchased with funds provided by an Anonymous donor and a gift of the artist

'foreign residence' – back to my homeland to add another level of complexity to my work on this subject. This enabled me to reflect further on space – personal, collective, national, cultural – as well as on the terms 'origin' and 'original' as in that which is secondary and/or a copy.

Seoul Home… is about carrying the personal space of my childhood memories with me, and taking my nostalgia into the space where I currently live. It addresses issues of separation, migration, loss and longing. The piece, *348 West 22nd Street, Apt. A, New York, N.Y. 10011 at Rodin Gallery, Seoul/Tokyo Opera City Art Gallery/Serpentine Gallery, London/Biennale of Sydney/ Seattle Art Museum* (2000), based upon my New York apartment, is about the present. The transporting of the space in which I currently live into the space that I left behind shows my desire to overcome or decrease the geographical and cultural distances between the two spaces: the one from which I originated and the one where I am now.

This show also travelled to Japan where I later added the pink fabric version of the corridor leading to my apartment. *The Perfect Home*, when eventually complete, will combine all the fabric pieces that I have made into one large complex. My Korean fabric house, New York apartment and even my studio are going to be connected by way of a fabric corridor that has five doors. For example, you will be able to enter my 'apartment' and go into my 'Korean house' through one of those doors.

LC You once said that you turned to making architectural pieces as a 'desperate gesture' in order to find a way to relate to your new surroundings in the United States. Is it true to say that you experienced the cultural dislocation not intellectually but physically as a change in the way you related to your body?

D-HS I felt that I was granted a new body when I came to America. I was dropped into a strange, foreign space. I felt like I didn't know how long my arms were or how tall I was. I tried to find ways to relate to myself in this new environment, and that is how I began literally measuring space.

LC You had to find a way to make a bridge in order to reconcile yourself to this new state of displacement. It seems that you were adjusting to spaces that had no association with your history or memories. Were you also attempting to build a cultural bridge?

D-HS The way various cultures manipulate architectural spaces are very different. I always say the 'scale' is different. That is perhaps the most obvious distinction between the way in which Eastern and Western cultures define space.

In Western buildings, you separate public and private space with a solid wall. This means you have more walls in Western culture. There are no walls in the building in which I grew up in Korea. It is all doors and windows. The apertures are covered with translucent rice paper that transmits light.

LC In a typical Korean house, the apertures are removable sliding doors that separate interior spaces so that their uses can be constantly altered. Even the furniture is portable. The rice-paper doors suggest tissue-like membranes.

D-HS Yes, Korean architecture is very porous. While you are sitting or sleeping in the room, you can hear everything inside and outside. You feel like you are in the middle of nature. In American

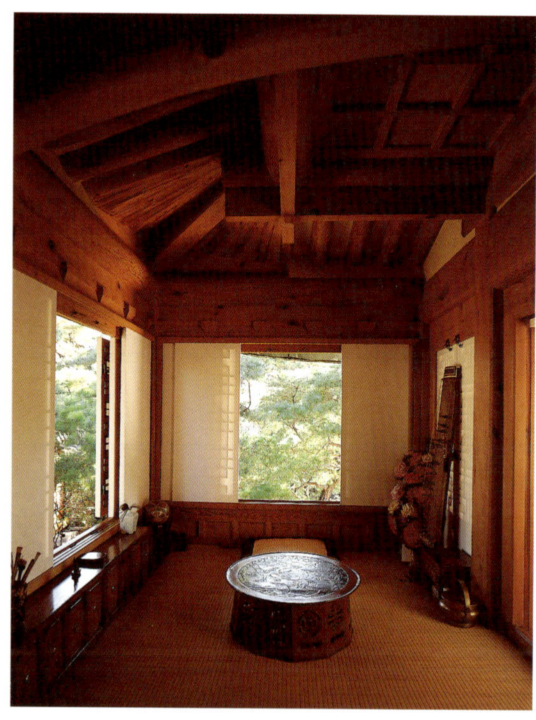

The house of Do-Ho Suh's parents,
Min-Za Chung and Se-Ok Suh (interior)

suburbs you have houses surrounded by 'nature'. When you enter the house, there's a separation between the two. In a Korean house you can hear the raindrops and the animals.

LC So, you can also hear the sounds of other people in the house?

D-HS Yes, there is much less privacy in a Korean architectural structure. But, at the same time, the walls around one's house define a family's boundaries. Typically, they are like layers of walled spaces you pass through before you actually go to your room. There is a courtyard in the centre and a series of interlocking cubes going around the perimeter. A street would run around the building.

LC The fabrics you use are both diaphanous and porous, and the way you layer them often creates shadows. Does your use of fabric reflect the symbiotic relationship between the external and internal spaces you have described in Korean architecture?

D-HS It was very natural for me to use fabric as a basis for my work. It is a particularly translucent material, like rice paper which is an integral part of architecture in Korea. I remember seeing through the rice-paper screen windows of our house in Korea, with the shadows of bamboo leaves blowing in the wind and lit by the reflection of a full moon. I could also smell the pine trees and the fragrance of plum blossoms through the screens.

I want my work to blend with the environment it finds itself in, to become part of the architecture

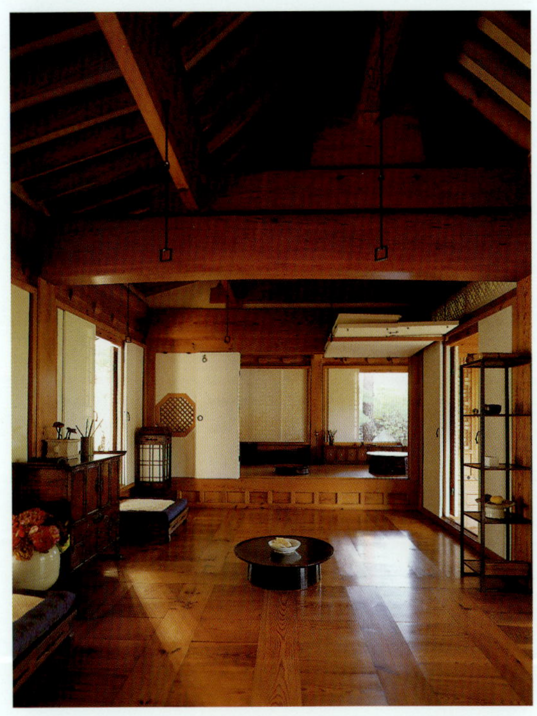

The house of Do-Ho Suh's parents, Min-Za Chung and Se-Ok Suh (interior)

that surrounds it. When I decided to use fabric I was also thinking about traditional Asian painting. Rice paper is a very porous material. It absorbs ink, unlike canvas onto which paint is applied. In the Western painting tradition, no matter how long you spend painting or how thickly you apply paint on the canvas what you're going to see is just the last layer of paint. Rice paper is made out of several layers. The brushstrokes of ink penetrate the paper.

LC The image is actually embedded in the material.

D-HS It is ambiguous whether the image is actually on the surface or in the paper, and this is one of the important differences between Western and Eastern painting. The framer laminates the paper with another paper to back it up, so the image becomes more vivid. One of my art teachers in Korea told me that master framers can slice the layers of paper so that you can have several originals. I do not know if this is true or not but it is a story that appeals to me.

LC That's like peeling away layers of skin.

D-HS I connect this to the idea of making a fabric house with the many layers that the viewer must pass through.

LC How many of the details in *Seoul Home...* are the same as the patterned decoration of your childhood house in Seoul?

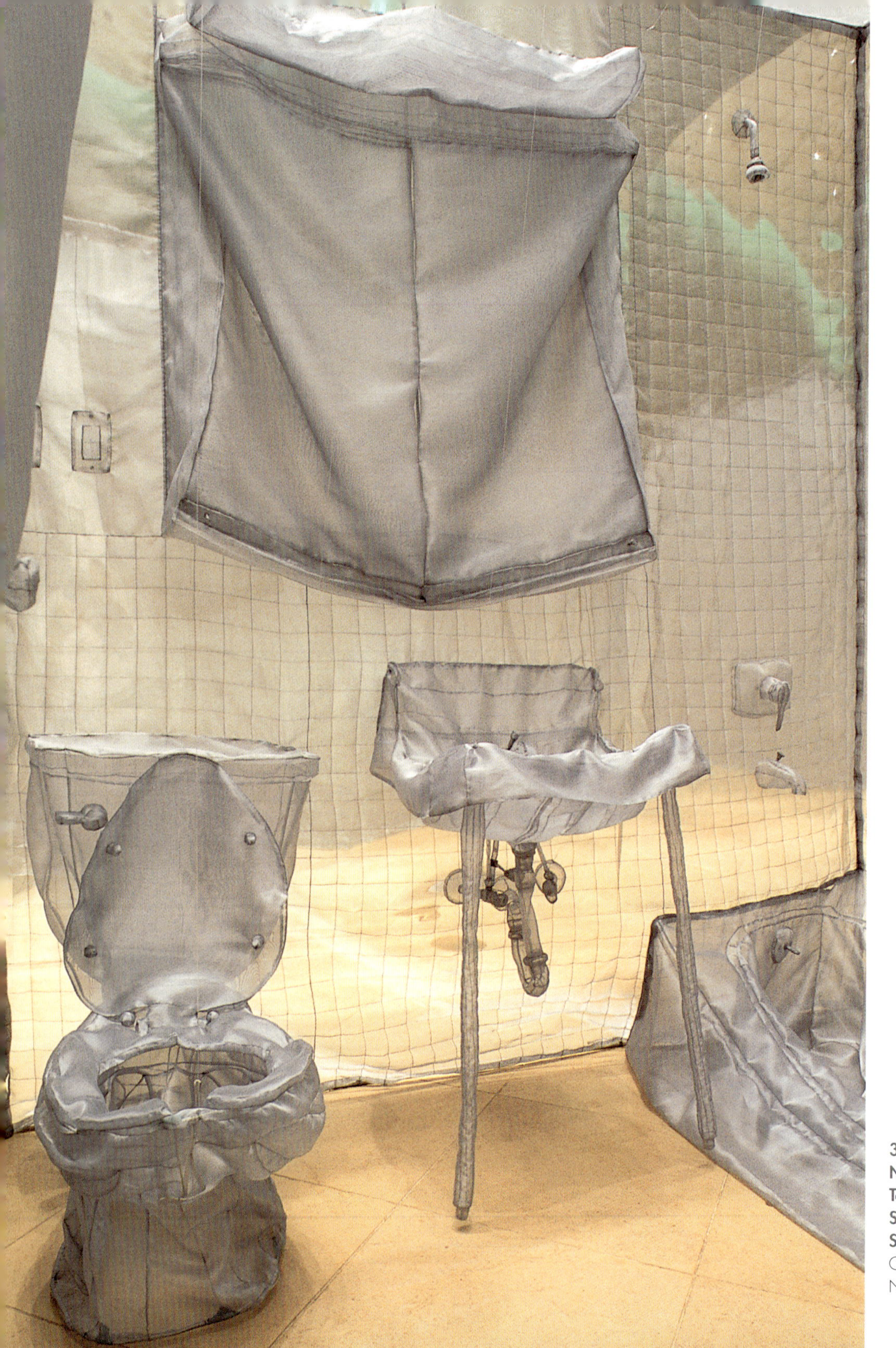

348 West 22nd St., Apt. A, New York, NY 10011 at Rodin Gallery, Seoul/ Tokyo Opera City Art Gallery/ Serpentine Gallery, London/Biennale of Sydney/Seattle Art Museum (detail) 2000
Courtesy of the artist and Lehman Maupin, New York

D-HS It's very precise. Some of the details capture exactly the carved geometric decorations on the house. I used magenta thread for stitches. This element relates to the vocabulary of costume-making, as in traditional Korean costume. I consider my pieces to be clothing for the space, and that is why I use a lot of traditional costume elements like ornaments.

LC Your mother is considered an expert on traditional Korean costume. Did she help you with the project? Did she teach you different stitches that are common in Korean dressmaking?

D-HS I was already somewhat familiar with traditional sewing techniques through my mother, but I didn't know how to create them. My mother used all of her resources to assist me. She knows master pattern-makers and dressmakers, who are all old ladies.

LC When she went to see these traditional Korean seamstresses, she must have described your work to them as contemporary art. Did you speak with them yourself about your work?

D-HS At first, it was hard to explain my project because they did not have any experience of this kind of art. Nonetheless, they got really excited about the project of trying to 'dress' a room. I stressed to them that we were making sculpture. The actual sewing was done together. I sewed the piece with the seamstresses.

LC Sewing and dressmaking are traditionally associated with women's labour. How much meaning should one attach to this reference?

D-HS For me, dressmaking is like architecture. When you expand this idea of clothing as a space, it becomes an inhabitable structure, a building, a house made of fabric. I covered everything with the fabric and measured very precisely in order to make the shape appear as a house. In the end, the process came closer to industrial design and architecture than to dressmaking.

LC One of the art historical references that readily comes to mind in looking at the soft sculpture details in works such as *348 West 22nd St....* is Claes Oldenburg. Do you feel your work shares an affinity with his?

D-HS I was definitely aware of superficial connections to Oldenburg because of my use of fabric to create 'soft' sculpture, but what makes my work different is that it is intended to be transportable. It is like transporting space. I am interested in portable site-specificity.

LC Oldenburg, like other artists of his generation playing with site-specificity, was interested primarily in how context invigorates the presence of a piece and adds new meaning to our experience of it. Cultural difference had very little to do with his work. Your spaces explore how our identity is shaped by the spaces we inhabit, but also how those spaces are shaped by who we are.

Unlike Oldenburg's works, yours are nomadic. They are not, strictly speaking, site specific. Their meaning migrates as they move from place to place. Creating nomadic spaces has enabled you to maintain your relationship with the spaces that most define you, no matter where you go. Another artist who creates nomadic works is Rirkrit Tiravanija. How would you characterize the difference between the spirit of your nomadic works and his?

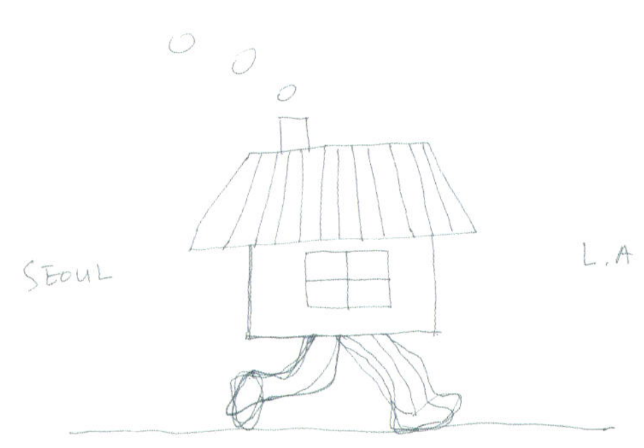

Seoul Home/L.A. Home 1999
Collection Estēe Lauder Companies

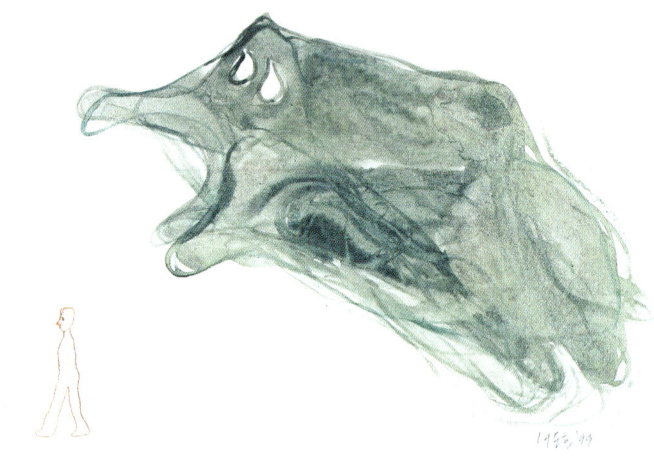

Haunting House 1999
Collection Estēe Lauder Companies

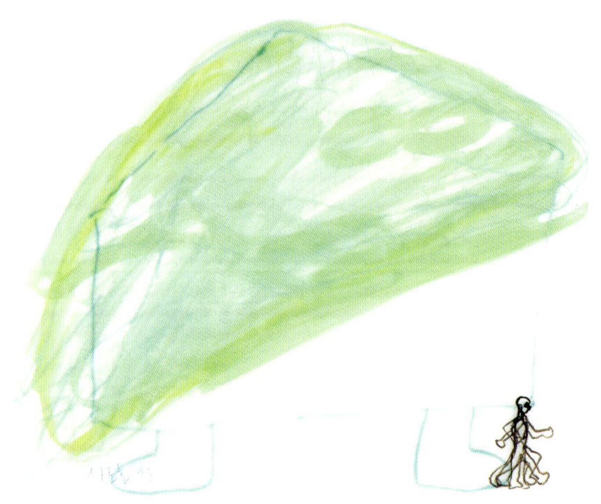

My House 1999
Collection Barbara Goldfarb

My Country 1999
Collection Barbara Goldfarb

D-HS Rirkrit's nomadic works are offerings. He is extremely generous in the ways he invites viewers to interact with his work.
LC Yes, he has offered visitors to his exhibitions ways to activate his work. Viewers have choices when they interact with your work, too.
D-HS When Rirkrit reconstructed his New York apartment in Cologne at the Kunstverein, he offered his private space as a public domain. But to be honest, I feel my project is kind of selfish. It's a need that I have to fulfil. I discovered that when my piece was shown in the *Greater New York* exhibition in New York at P.S.1. There were so many people at the opening standing underneath the piece looking up into it, that I realized this very personal space had become a very public entity.
LC Did you feel as though they had invaded your psychological space?
D-HS In a way, yes. I had an unexpected mixture of feelings. My brother, who happens to be an architect, was there and he felt exactly the same way. There was the house in which we grew up, and we could remember everything about it, down to the marks on the wall that had occurred over time. We stood there remembering all those things, while other viewers were carefully examining the piece.
LC The space had become something else to the viewers.
D-HS Exactly, and it gave me a strange feeling.
LC What is really interesting is how the piece gets transformed. The viewer brings to the work his or her own set of personal, social, and architectural reference points.
D-HS They don't necessarily have to know about all the specific references to Korean culture and architecture. The United States is a country of immigrants and Americans are always on the move. I think anyone who has left home and moved around understands the act of crossing boundaries.
LC Ultimately, the relationship of the piece to the original house is primarily relevant and necessary to you. It seems to have provided a sense of security in a foreign place.
D-HS While I was making *Seoul Home*... I actually made a drawing of a house that's a parachute. A paratrooper is descending from the sky with the house-parachute over his head.
LC Does the drawing depict a Western house or a Korean house?
D-HS It is a Korean house. This drawing is about my feeling of displacement. Paratroopers are soldiers dropped into enemy territory. They have to survive using any means. They certainly cannot survive without the parachutes that allow them to land on the ground softly so they don't crash.
LC This suggests that you were compelled to make *The Perfect Home* pieces in order to survive your displacement from Korea to the West.
D-HS Yes, my transportable Korean house has been my parachute.

Footnote

1 For an in-depth discussion of the historical architecture that is part of Suh's family living complex, see Carol Lutfy, 'An Artist's Seoul Asylum', *Architectural Digest* (August 1994): 111–21.

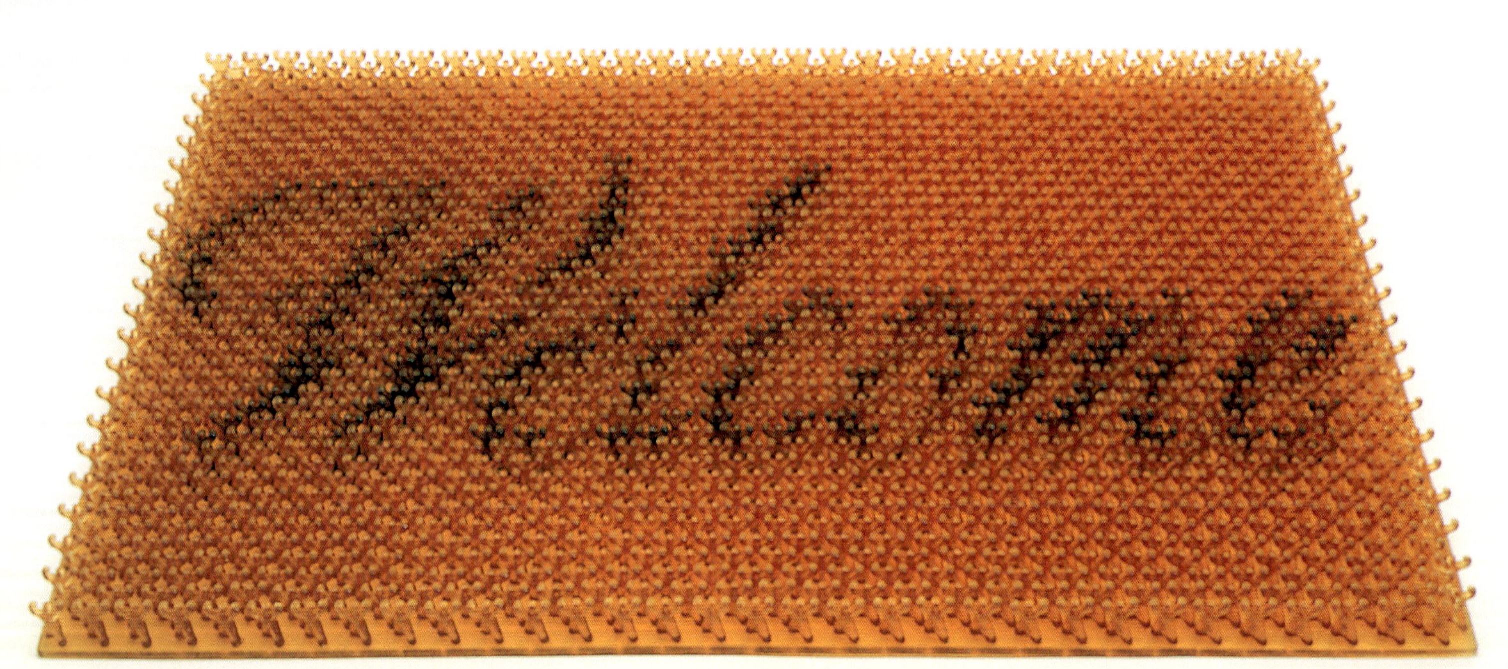

Doormat: Welcome (Amber) 2000
Courtesy of the artist and Lehmann Maupin Gallery, New York

Works in the Exhibition

High School Uni-Form 1996
Fabric, plastic, stainless steel, casters
60 parts: overall dimensions
149.9 x 215.9 x 365.8 cm
59 x 85 x 144 inches
Edition 1/3
Collection David Teiger

High School Uni-Face 1997
Computer-generated colour photograph
152.4 x 127 cm
60 x 50 inches
Edition 1/6
Courtesy of the artist and
Lehmann Maupin Gallery, New York

Floor 1997–2000
PVC figures, glass plates, Phenolic sheets, polyurethane resin
Serpentine Gallery: 25 modules
Seattle Art Museum: 40 modules
Each module: 100 x 100 cm
Each module: 39 x 39 inches
Courtesy of the artist and
Lehmann Maupin Gallery, New York

Haunting House 1999
Ink and coloured pencil on paper
27.9 x 36.2 cm
11 x 14 ¼ inches
Collection Estēe Lauder Companies

Seoul Home/L.A. Home 1999
Ink on paper
27.9 x 36.2 cm
11 x 14 ¼ inches
Collection Estēe Lauder Companies

My House 1999
Ink on paper
27.9 x 35.6 cm
11 x 14 inches
Collection Barbara Goldfarb

My Country 1999
Ink on paper
27.9 x 35.6 cm
11 x 14 inches
Collection Barbara Goldfarb

Seoul Home/L.A. Home/New York Home/ Baltimore Home/London Home/Seattle Home 1999
Silk
378.5 x 609.6 x 609.6 cm
149 x 240 x 240 inches
The Museum of Contemporary Art,
Los Angeles
Purchased with funds provided by an
Anonymous donor and a gift of the artist

Doormat: Welcome (Amber) 2000
Polyurethane rubber
127 x 213.4 cm
50 x 84 inches
Edition 2/3
Courtesy of the artist and
Lehmann Maupin Gallery, New York

348 West 22nd St., Apt. A, New York, NY 10011 at Rodin Gallery, Seoul/Tokyo Opera City Art Gallery/Serpentine Gallery, London/Biennale of Sydney/Seattle Art Museum 2000
Translucent nylon
430 x 690 x 245 cm
169 x 272 x 96 ½ inches
Edition 2/3
Collection Ninah and Michael Lynne
(Exhibited only at the Serpentine Gallery)

348 West 22nd St., Apt. A, New York, NY 10011 at Rodin Gallery, Seoul/Tokyo Opera City Art Gallery/Serpentine Gallery, London/Biennale of Sydney/Seattle Art Museum 2000
Translucent nylon
430 x 690 x 245 cm
169 x 272 x 96 ½ inches
Edition 1/3
Courtesy of the artist and
Lehmann Maupin, New York
(Exhibited only at the Seattle Art Museum)

Who Am We? (Multi) 2000
Four-colour offset wallpaper
Each sheet: 61 x 91.4 cm
Each sheet: 24 x 36 inches
Courtesy of the artist and
Lehmann Maupin Gallery, New York

348 West 22nd St., Apt. A, New York, NY 10011 at Rodin Gallery, Seoul/Tokyo Opera City Art Gallery/Serpentine Gallery, London/Biennale of Sydney/Seattle Art Museum (corridor) 2001
Translucent nylon
168 x 1240 x 245 cm
169 x 690 x 96 ½ inches
Edition 2/3
Courtesy of the artist and
Lehmann Maupin Gallery, New York
(Exhibited only at the Serpentine Gallery)

348 West 22nd St., Apt. A, New York, NY 10011 at Rodin Gallery, Seoul/Tokyo Opera City Art Gallery/Serpentine Gallery, London/Biennale of Sydney/Seattle Art Museum (corridor) 2001
Translucent nylon
168 x 1240 x 245 cm
169 x 690 x 96 ½ inches
Edition 1/3
Courtesy of the artist and
Lehmann Maupin Gallery, New York
(Exhibited only at the Seattle Art Museum)

Some/One 2001
Stainless steel military dog tags, nickel plated copper sheets, steel structure, glass fibre reinforced resin, rubber sheets
Overall dimensions variable; figure:
205 x 320 cm diameter
81 x 126 inches diameter
Edition 2/3
Collection of the Samsung Museum of
Modern Art, Seoul, Korea
Courtesy of Lehmann Maupin Gallery,
New York

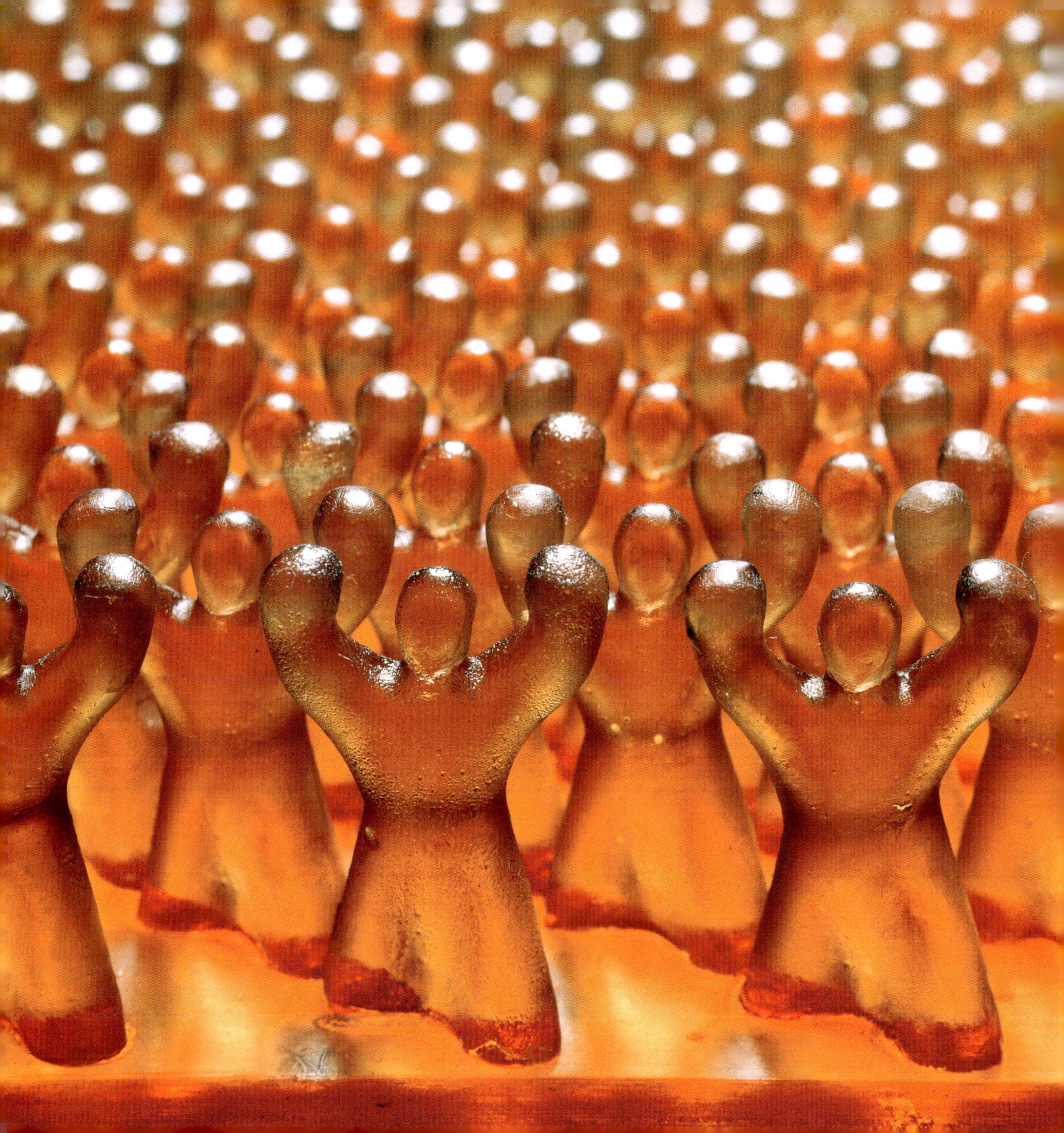

Do-Ho Suh

Born in Seoul, Korea, 1962

Lives and works in New York, New York

1997
M.F.A. Sculpture, Yale University School of Art, New Haven, Connecticut

1994
B.F.A. Painting, Rhode Island School of Design, Providence, Rhode Island

1993
Skowhegan School of Painting and Sculpture, Skowhegan, Maine

1987
M.F.A and B.F.A. Oriental Painting, Seoul National University, Seoul, Korea

Solo Exhibitions

2002
The Perfect Home, Kemper Contemporary Art Museum, Kansas City, Missouri

Do-Ho Suh, Serpentine Gallery, London, and Seattle Art Museum, Seattle, Washington (catalogue)

2001
Do-Ho Suh: Some/One, Whitney Museum of American Art at Philip Morris, New York, New York (brochure)

2000
Do-Ho Suh, Lehmann Maupin Gallery, New York, New York

1999
Seoul Home/L.A. Home, Korean Cultural Center, Los Angeles, California

Sight-Seeing, NTT InterCommunication Center, Tokyo, Japan (catalogue)

Selected Group Exhibitions

2002
The Fourth Asia Pacific Triennial of Contemporary Art, Queensland Art Gallery, Brisbane, Australia

(The World May Be) Fantastic, Biennale of Sydney, Sydney, Australia

Sculptura 02, Falkenberg, Sweden

2001
Lunapark: Contemporary Art from Korea, Württembergischer Kunstverein Stuttgart, Stuttgart, Germany (catalogue)

Everybody Now, Bertha and Karl Leubsdorf Art Gallery, Hunter College, New York, New York (catalogue)

Korean Pavilion (with Michael Joo), La Biennale di Venezia, The 49th International Art Exhibition, Venice, Italy (catalogue)

Plateau of Humankind, La Biennale di Venezia, The 49th International Art Exhibition, Venice, Italy

Made in Asia, Duke University Art Museum, Durham, North Carolina (catalogue)

About Face, The Museum of Modern Art, New York, New York

Subject Plural: Crowds in Contemporary Art, Houston Contemporary Arts Museum, Houston, Texas (catalogue)

Currents in Korean Contemporary Art II, Hong Kong Art Centre, Hong Kong

BodySpace, The Baltimore Museum of Art, Baltimore, Maryland (catalogue)

Uniforme, Ordine e Disordine (*Uniform, Order and Disorder*), Stazione Leopolda, Florence, Italy (travelled to P.S.1 Contemporary Art Center, Long Island City, New York) (catalogue)

Greater New York, P.S.1 Contemporary Art Center, Long Island City, New York

Koreamericakorea, Artsonje Center, Seoul, Korea and Artsonje Art Museum, Kyongju, Korea (catalogue)

Open Ends, The Museum of Modern Art, New York, New York

My Home is Yours. Your Home is Mine. Rodin Gallery, the Samsung Museum of Modern Art, Seoul, Korea (travelled to Tokyo Opera City Art Gallery, Tokyo, Japan) (catalogue)

Currents in Korean Contemporary Art I, Taipei Fine Arts Museum, Taipei, Taiwan

Trippy World, Baron/Boisante, New York, New York

The Self, Absorbed, Bellevue Art Museum, Bellevue, Washington

Uniform, Center for Curatorial Studies, Bard College, Annandale-on-Hudson, New York

1998
Cross-Cultural Voices: Asian American Artists, University Art Gallery, Staller Center for the Arts, State University of New York at Stony Brook, New York (catalogue)

Editions '98, Brooke Alexander Editions, New York, New York

Beyond the Monument, MetroTech Center Commons, Brooklyn, New York

Do-Ho Suh/Royce Weatherly, Gavin Brown's Enterprise, New York, New York

Promenade in Asia 1997, Shiseido Gallery, Tokyo, Japan

Techno Seduction, The Cooper Union for the Advancement of Science and Art, New York, New York

Doormat: Welcome (Amber) (detail) 2000
Courtesy of the artist and Lehmann Maupin Gallery, New York

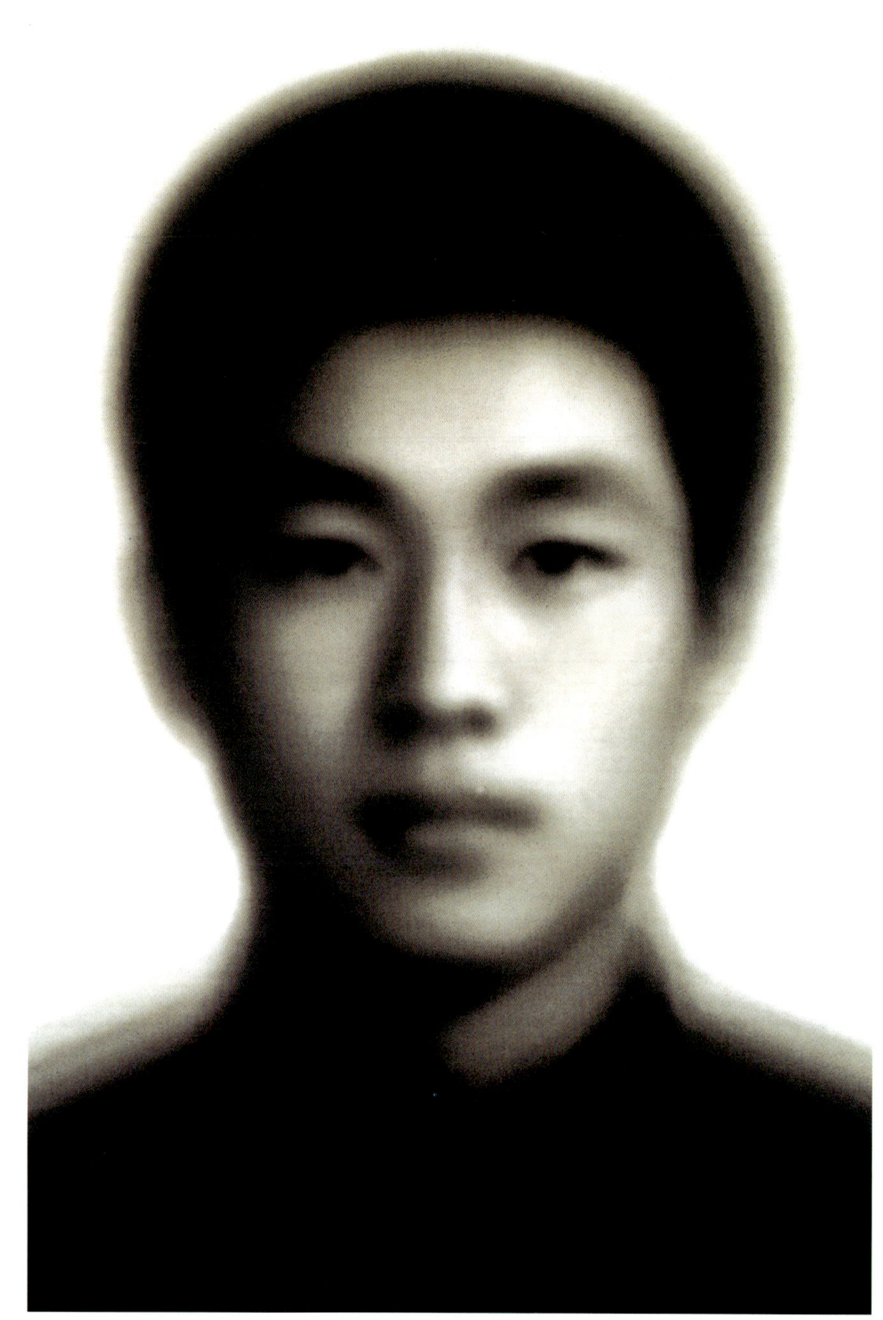

High School Uni-Face 1997
Courtesy of the artist and Lehmann Maupin Gallery, New York

Window Show, Gallery Hyundai, Seoul, Korea

Art at Home, Seomi Gallery, Seoul, Korea

Arcos da Lapa, Rio de Janeiro, Brazil

1995
6 Artists Now, Gallery Hyundai, Seoul, Korea

1990
The Grouping Youth 1990, The National Museum of Contemporary Art, Kwachon, Korea

1989
20th São Paulo International Biennial, São Paulo, Brazil

Selected Bibliography

2002
Clifford, Katie. 'A Soldier's Story.' *ArtNews*, January, pp. 102–5.

Richard, Frances. 'The Art of Do-Ho Suh: Home in the World.' *Artforum*, January, pp. 114–8.

2001
Christov-Barkagiev, Carolyn. 'And the winner is.' *Tema Celeste*, Summer, pp. 38–43.

Ellegood, Anne. 'La Biennale de Venise.' *artpress*, June, pp. 34–9.

Malhotra, Priya. 'Do-Ho Suh.' *Tema Celeste*, January/February, pp. 52–5.

Liu, Jenny. 'Do-Ho Suh.' *frieze*, January/February, pp. 118–9.

Harper, Glenn. 'Do-Ho Suh.' *Sculpture*, January/February, pp. 62–3.

2000
Leffingwell, Edward. 'Do-Ho Suh at Lehmann Maupin.' *Art in America*, November, p. 162.

Cotter, Holland. 'Do-Ho Suh.' *The New York Times*, September 29, p. 31.

Dannatt, Adrian. 'Little people at Lehmann Maupin.' *The Art Newspaper*, No. 106, September, p. 78.

Dailey, Meghan. 'Greater New York.' *artpress*, July/August, pp. 66–7.

Kino, Carol. 'The Emergent Factor'. *Art in America*, July, pp. 44–9.

1999
Kwon, Miwon. 'Emerging Artist: Do-Ho Suh – Uniform Appearance.' *Art* (Seoul, Korea). December, pp. 78–80.

Lazar, Julie. 'Emerging Artist: Do-Ho Suh – Seoul Home/L.A. Home.' *Art* (Seoul, Korea), December, p. 81.

Kim, Young-Il. 'About Cover: Do-Ho Suh.' *Art* (Seoul, Korea), December, pp. 18–9.

1998
Kwon, Miwon. 'Uniform Appearance.' *frieze*, January/February, pp. 68–9.

1996
Chun, Seung-Bo. 'Artists at Work: Do-Ho Suh.' *Gana Art* (Seoul, Korea) March, pp. 104–5.

Barros, Andre Luiz, 'Os Arcos "mágicos" da Lapa.' *Jornal do Brasil* (Rio de Janeiro, Brazil), November 8, p. 6.

Miranda, Claudia, 'Novas cores para os Arcos.' *Tribuna* (Rio de Janeiro, Brazil), November 5, p. 6.

Trustees of the Serpentine Gallery

Lord Palumbo *Chairman*
Felicity Waley-Cohen &
Barry Townsley
Co-Vice Chairmen
Marcus Boyle *Treasurer*
Patricia Bickers
Mark Booth
Roger Bramble
Marco Compagnoni
David Fletcher
Zaha Hadid
Isaac Julien
Joan Smith
Colin Tweedy

Council, Patrons, Benefactors and Supporters of the Serpentine Gallery

Council of the Serpentine Gallery
Rob Hersov *Chairman*
Mr and Mrs Harry Blain
Kim Hersov
And members of the Council who wish to remain anonymous

Emeritus Benefactor
Edwin C. Cohen and The Blessing Way Foundation

Honorary Patron
Anthony Podesta, Podesta/Mattoon.com, Washington DC

Honorary Benefactors
Gavin Aldred
Mark and Lauren Booth
Ivor Braka
Noam and Geraldine Gottesman
Catherine and Pierre Lagrange
Stig Larsen
George and Angie Loudon
Mrs Robin Heller Moss and
Mr Stephen A. Webb
Lord Rothschild
Peter Simon

Patrons
Charles Asprey Esq
Simon Bakewell and Cheri Phillips
Charles and Léonie Booth-Clibborn
Frances and John Bowes
Jonathan and Vanessa Cameron
Mr and Mrs Cuniberti
Fine Family Foundation
Mr and Mrs Edwin Fox
David and Danielle Ganek
Sir Ronald Grierson
Mr and Mrs Michael Hue-Williams
Rachel Lehmann and David Maupin
Mr and Mrs Peter Marano
Christian and Cherise Mouiex
Michael Ringier
Alan and Joan Smith
Laura and Barry Townsley
Robert and Felicity Waley-Cohen
Poju and Anita Zabludowicz

Benefactors
Heinz and Simone Ackermans
Max Alexander and Anna Bateson
Alan and Charlotte Artus
James M. Bartos
Anne Best
Roger and Beverley Bevan
David and Janice Blackburn
Anthony and Gisela Bloom
John and Jean Botts
Amber and James Bowles
Marcus Boyle
Vanessa Branson
Benjamin Brown
Mr and Mrs Charles Brown
John and Susan Burns
Jonathon P. Carroll
Monkey Chambers
Mr and Mrs Giuseppe Ciardi
Michèle Claudel-Maier
Dr and Mrs David Cohen
Sir Ronald and Lady Cohen
Sadie Coles
Carole Conrad
Simon Copsey
Loraine da Costa
Cathy Curan
Linda and Ronald F. Daitz
Ellynne Dec and Andrea Prat
Neil Duckworth
Lance Entwistle
Mr and Mrs Mark Fenwick
Maren and Konstantin Fiedler
Harry and Ruth Fitzgibbons
David and Jane Fletcher
Bruce and Janet Flohr
Forward Publishing
Eric and Louise Franck
James Freedman and Anna Kissin
Albert and Lyn Fuss
David Gill
Barbara Gladstone
Glovers Solicitors
Dimitri J. Goulandris
Francesco Grana and Simona Fantinelli
Richard and Odile Grogan
Richard and Linda Grosse
The Bryan Guinness Charitable Trust
Philip Gumuchdjian
Abel G. Halpern and Helen Chung-Halpern
Mr and Mrs Rupert Hambro
Mr and Mrs Antony Harbour
Susan Harris
Michael and Danah Hatt
Mr and Mrs Rick Hayward
Thomas Healy and Fred Hochberg
Paul Hobson
Montague Hurst Charitable Trust
Mr Michael and Lady Miranda Hutchinson
Nicola Jacobs and Tony Schlesinger
Susie Jubb
John Kaldor and Naomi Milgrom
Howard and Linda Karshan
King Sturge & Co
James and Clare Kirkman
Tim and Dominique Kirkman
Mr and Mrs Charles Kirwan-Taylor
Mickey and Jeanne Klein
The Landau Foundation
Mr and Mrs Simon Lee
Barbara Lloyd and Judy Collins
Peder Lund
Steve and Fran Magee
Karim Manji
The Lord and Lady Marks
Catherine Martin
James and Viviane Mayor
Warren and Victoria Miro
Susan and Claus Moehlmann
Crissij van den Munckhof
Mr and Mrs Rupert Nathan
Marian and Hugh Nineham
Georgia Oetker
Ophiucus SA
Mr and Mrs Nicholas Oppenheim
Linda Pace
Desmond Page and Asun Gelardin
Dominic Palfreyman
Midge and Simon Palley
Kathrine Palmer
William Palmer
Andrew Partridge
Julia Peyton-Jones
Trevor Pickett
George and Carolyn Pincus
Ben and Georgie Pincus
Nyda and Oliver Prenn
Mathew and Angela Prichard
Michael Rich
John and Jill Ritblat
Jacqueline and Nicholas Roe
James Roundell and Bona Montagu
Rolf and Maryan Sachs
Dr and Mrs Mortimer Sackler
Michael and Julia Samuel
The Lily and Marcus Sieff Charitable Trust
Martin and Elise Smith
Sotheby's
Bina and Philippe von Stauffenberg
Ian and Mercedes Stoutzker
The Thames Wharf Charity
Christian and Sarah von Thun-Hohenstein
Mrs Britt Tidelius
Constanze von Unruh
David and Emma Verey
Mr and Mrs Ludovic de Walden
Audrey Wallrock
Anthony Weldon
Lord and Lady John Wellesley
Katherine Wenning and Michael Dennis
Charles and Kathryn Wickham
Robin Wight and Anastasia Alexander
Richard and Astrid Wolman
Chad Wollen and Sian Davies
Andrzej and Jill Zarzycki
And Benefactors who wish to remain anonymous

Founding Corporate Benefactor
Bloomberg

Platinum Corporate Benefactors
Alphabet
c-quential, an Arthur D. Little company
Omni Colour Presentations
Selfridges & Co
UBS Private Banking
Vertu
Yves Saint Laurent Rive Gauche

Gold Corporate Benefactors
Coutts Contemporary Art Foundation
Digital Video Systems Ltd
Hydro Aluminium
Korean Air
Shanghai Tang
Sony Broadcast & Professional
Venture3

The Serpentine Gallery Education Programme is supported by
The Arthur Andersen Foundation
The Bridge House Estates Trust Fund
The Diana, Princess of Wales Memorial Fund
The Woo Charitable Foundation

With additional generous support from
John Lyon's Charity
The Paul Hamlyn Foundation

And kind assistance from
The Baring Foundation
The Calouste Gulbenkian Foundation
The David Cohen Family Charitable Trust
The Goldsmith's Company
J. Paul Getty Jr. Charitable Trust
The Mercers' Company
The Worshipful Company of Grocers

Seattle Art Museum Board Officers and Board of Trustees

Seattle Art Museum Board Officers

Chairman: Jon Shirley
President: Susan Brotman
Vice President: Charles Wright
Vice President: Christine Nicolov
Secretary: Watson Blair
Treasurer: Stanley Savage

Seattle Art Museum Board of Trustees

Active
Margaret Allison
Eve Alvord
Rosa Ayer
Frank Bayley
Watson Blair
Jeffrey Brotman
Susan Brotman
Steven A. Clifford
Oliver Cobb
Brad Davis
Patrick Dineen
Barney A. Ebsworth
Pamela Ebsworth
Margery Friedlander
José Gaitán
P. Raaze Garrison
Vicki Griffin
Helen Gurvich
Betty Hedreen
Ray Ifert
Mary Ketcham Kerr
Janet Ketcham
Linda Killinger
Christina A. Lockwood
Barbara Malone
David E. Maryatt
Sally Maryatt
Dipti Mathur
Belle Maxwell
Herman McKinney
Charles H. Mitchell
John A. Moga
Scott Morris
Sally Neukom
Assunta Ng
Christine Nicolov
Doug Norberg
Linda Nordstrom
Sally B. Nordstrom
Ruth Nutt
Brooks G. Ragen
Constance W. Rice
Elizabeth Roberts
Sam Rubinstein
Faye Sarkowsky
Stanley Savage
Thomas E. Schick
Roberta Sherman
Jon Shirley
Kayla Skinner
Jairus Stratton
Winifred Stratton
Robert Strong
Althea Stroum
Daphne Tang
Dean D. Thornton
Griffith Way
Richard Weisman
Charles Wright
Virginia Wright
Ann P. Wyckoff

Ex-Officio
Ann Barwick
Bruce Bentley
Katie Bunn-Marcuse
Christine Burgoyne
JoAnn Cowan
Billy Howard
Jan Kumasaka
Mary Rae Mattix
Kim Richter
Elizabeth Rummage
Peter Steinbrueck
Paul Toliver
Shirley Younglove

Honorary
Nancy Alvord
Robert M. Arnold
Thomas Barwick
Richard P. Cooley
Jane Davis
P. Cameron DeVore
Robert Dootson
Anne Gerber
Marshall Hatch
John H. Hauberg
James C. Hawkanson
C. Calvert Knudsen
Margaret Perthou-Taylor
Phillip E. Renshaw
Mary Robinson
Langdon Simons
Bagley Wright

This catalogue is published to accompany the exhibition

Do-Ho Suh

Serpentine Gallery, London 23 April – 26 May 2002
Seattle Art Museum downtown and Seattle Asian Art Museum at Volunteer Park 10 August – 1 December 2002

Curated by Lisa G. Corrin, Deputy Director of Art/Jon and Mary Shirley Curator of Modern and Contemporary Art, Seattle Art Museum and former Chief Curator of the Serpentine Gallery, London

Prepared and published by the Serpentine Gallery, London, and the Seattle Art Museum, Seattle, Washington

Designed by Herman Lelie, London
Typeset by Stefania Bonelli, London
Printed in Great Britain by PJ Print, London

Serpentine Gallery
Kensington Gardens
London W2 3XA
Telephone +44 (0)20 7402 6075
Fax +44 (0)20 7402 4103
www.serpentinegallery.org

Serpentine Gallery

Seattle Art Museum
100 University Street,
Seattle, Washington 98101

Seattle Asian Art Museum
1400 Prospect Street
Volunteer Park
Seattle, Washington 98112

Telephone 1–206–625–8900
Fax 1–206–654–3135
www.seattleartmuseum.org

SAM

© 2002 Serpentine Gallery, London; the Seattle Art Museum, Seattle; and the authors
All works by Do-Ho Suh © 2002 the artist

All rights reserved. No part of this publication may be reproduced, stored in a retrieval system or transmitted in any form or by any means, electronic, mechanical, photocopying, recording or otherwise without the prior permission of the publisher.

In London, *Do-Ho Suh* is sponsored by Bloomberg

Bloomberg

In Seattle, the exhibition is supported by the Anne Gerber Exhibition Endowment Fund. Generous support also provided by Maryann and Henry James and contributors to the Annual Fund. *Deepening the Dialogue*, an initiative funded by the Wallace-Reader's Digest Funds, is a key component of this exhibition, strengthening SAM's programming and community partnerships.

ISBN 1-870814-56-8 (Serpentine Gallery, London)
ISBN 0-932216-55-2 (Seattle Art Museum)

Photographic credits:
Nakano Masataka, pp. 21, 24
Young-Il Kim, pp. 29, 34–35
© Min-Za Chung and Se-Ok Suh, pp. 29, 34–35
All photos courtesy of the artist and Lehmann Maupin, except above noted

Cover and frontispiece: **Some/One** 2001
Collection of the Samsung Museum of Modern Art, Seoul, Korea
Courtesy of Lehmann Maupin Gallery, New York